BALTIMORE DURING THE CIVIL WAR

Scott Sumpter Sheads

Daniel Carroll Toomey

For information about this and other titles, contact:
    Toomey Press
    P.O. Box 122
    Linthicum, Maryland 21090
    (410) 850-0831

Photographic Credits:
    D.C.T. Daniel Carroll Toomey
    All others indicated by specific source.

Book Design and Production:
    Cynthia Merrifield
    Merrifield Graphics and Publishing Service, Inc., Baltimore, MD

Printing:
    H. G. Roebuck & Son, Baltimore, MD

CONTENTS

This work is dedicated to

Jacob Melchoir Sheads, who served at Fort McHenry in 1935, and later as historian at Gettysburg National Military Park, 1937-1974.
From his "rebel cousin."
Scott Sumpter Sheads

and

Two long time residents of Baltimore
Anna Gertrude Toomey and Ruth Evelyn Silberzahn.
My two Moms.
Daniel Carroll Toomey

INTRODUCTION

To appreciate the events which occurred in Baltimore City during the Civil War one must understand its pre-war history. Baltimore Town did not begin to prosper until after the American Revolution. It was blessed not only with a good harbor, but with one that, thanks to the intrusion of the Chesapeake Bay on the continent, was 200 miles closer to the western markets than other ports located on or near the Atlantic coast. This was a tremendous advantage during the period of time when land transportation consisted of wagon trains and dirt roads. An advantage that with all the advancements of technology, was not lost until the later part of the twentieth century.

A second benefit to this geographic position was a city located on the fall line where fast moving rivers like the Patapsco River and Jones Falls could supply an abundance of water power for mills and factories. This combination of fresh water and a deep water port, also made Baltimore an ideal site for shipbuilding. Again the port supported this growth by drawing immigrants from western Europe to work in the factories and provided a means of shipping the manufactured goods to foreign markets.

The next step in the growth of the city was the founding of the Baltimore and Ohio Railroad in 1828. Far sighted men like Phillip Thomas, its first president, created a corporate giant that not only connected the Ohio Valley with the docks of Baltimore, but acted as a magnet for investment capital and new technologies. It was the Baltimore and Ohio Railroad that offered Samuel F. B. Morris the use of its right of way to run his experimental telegraph line that in time gave the railroad a dynamic management tool in the form of instant communication over long distances.

The first great landmark of the city was Federal Hill (previously named as Captain John Smith Hill for his log entry of the site in 1608) where Marylanders celebrated the ratification of the Federal Constitution in 1788. In 1797, the three separate communities of Jones Town, Baltimore Town and Fells Point were incorporated to form Baltimore City.

The defeat of the British during the War of 1812 gave Baltimore a near city-state pride in its celebrated defense of Fort McHenry in September 1814. The publication of "The Star-Spangled Banner" by Maryland attorney Francis Scott Key gave the city and nation its first

American icon — the United States Flag, a symbol of a new nation and a young maritime nation's flag, both nationalistic identities, not heretofore recognized. The return in 1815, of the war's most successful Baltimore privateer, the *Chasseur*, prompted the editor of the *Niles Weekly Register* to proclaim it "the pride of Baltimore."

That same year the cornerstone was laid for the Battle Monument dedicated to the 1814 Defenders on land donated by John Eager Howard. The monument and Fort McHenry were constantly linked to the identity of the city in the decades before the Civil War and were obvious symbols of defiance and suppression during the war years.

By 1860 Baltimore was the largest industrial city in the South and the third largest city in the United States. Three major railroads and an endless stream of sailing vessels traded its commerce over a major part of the country and the world. At the same time a flood of Irish and German immigrants during the 1850's combined with the industrialization of the city to undermine the institution of slavery. Baltimore City had a strong Southern social order with many ties to Virginia and the deep South. Yet, only in Southern Maryland did the plantation system of the colonial period remain unchanged.

Its population of 200,000 in 1860 contained 50,000 free blacks, the largest anywhere in the nation. Those still enslaved in the city were primarily house servants or in some way specially trained. In 1864 hundreds of Free Black males would join their still enslaved brothers to form six full regiments of U.S. Colored Troops which were recruited in Baltimore City and on both shores of the Chesapeake Bay.

When the war came in 1861, Maryland would be on the fault line of secession no matter which government its citizens voted to support. Baltimore City with its transportation and industrial assets would be a valuable prize to whichever side could control her. It is no wonder that all but the most heated firebrands waited until every avenue of compromise was exhausted before choosing sides in a war in which they had much to lose and very little to gain.

Never before have the people, places and events that occurred in this great city between the years 1860 and 1865 been presented in one continuous story. The authors now proudly tell that story in *Baltimore During the Civil War*.

Scott Sumpter Sheads   Daniel Carroll Toomey
Fort McHenry, Maryland   Linthicum, Maryland

(D.C.T.)

Battle Monument: Erected to the defenders of Baltimore during the War of 1812, it was the official symbol of the city and site of political rallies for decades before the war.

I

*P*EACE, *P*ROSPERITY, AND *P*OLITICS

*A*fter the Revolutionary War the commercial development of the city was linked to ship building and international trade. The Baltimore clipper, built more for war than peace, specialized during the War of 1812 as a privately armed vessel — a privateer. Its success against British merchantmen brought the Royal Navy to the Chesapeake Bay in 1814 to destroy Baltimore, what the *London Times* called "that nest of pirates." Only the successful defense of Fort McHenry in September 1814 prevented this from happening.[1]

In the aftermath of the battle the city was given a historic landmark, the Battle Monument, and a generation of veterans known as the "Old Defenders." Just as the War of 1812 had ended, the owners of the Brig

Chasseur sent her via Cape of Good Hope to Canton, China. She returned with the spices and exotic materials from the Far East, joining Baltimore with New England in this new area of economic opportunity.

Succeeding decades saw no local conflict. The founding of the Baltimore and Ohio Railroad brought more wealth and vitality to the city. The railroad linked the foreign markets of the world with the Ohio Valley and the western expansion of the young nation. The National Road, begun in 1810, now carried Baltimore goods across the Alleghenies to the Ohio River. All manner of raw material and finished products crossed its docks and bumped along the rails of one, two, and then three major railroads converging on the city. Business was managed to a great extent by trading firms such as Robert Garrett and Sons, and Robert F. Gilmor and Sons. Their success led to the creation of an elite merchant class in Baltimore City.

One lesson learned during the War of 1812 was that Fort McHenry was situated too close to the city to prevent damage from a naval bombardment. Like other maritime markets, Baltimore's dockyards and trades were expanding beyond these earlier shore defenses. As early as 1818, Sollers Point Flats, located four miles below the fort, was selected as an alternative site for a new fort. In 1847, construction was begun on a masonry pentagonal fort that was to be named after Charles Carroll of Carrollton. Brevet Colonel Robert E. Lee of the Army Corps of Engineers was assigned to Fort Carroll to supervise the project. It was not until the spring of 1849 that work began in earnest. Lee moved his family from Mount Vernon to a newly built three-story house at 908 Madison Avenue. It would be their residence for the next four years. His commitment to the project and skill as an engineer caused the stone and brick fortress to rise from the shoals four miles from the Chesapeake Bay.[2]

It was a five-sided structure resembling the soon to be famous Fort Sumter in the harbor of Charleston, South Carolina. In the spring of 1852 Lee received orders to report to West Point as superintendent of the United States Military Academy. Captain Henry Brewerton was in turn ordered from West Point to Baltimore to replace Lee at Fort Carroll. By 1860 enough of the fort had been completed to give the city a strong inner and outer harbor defense. This arrangement was very similar to the fortifications in Charleston. Unlike Charleston, however, the federal government was never forced to relinquish its control of Fort McHenry, thus keeping Fort Carroll from the fate and fame enjoyed by Fort Sumter in April of 1861.[3]

Close to the population center of the United States during the first half of the nineteenth century, Baltimore became home of the Democratic National Convention between 1832 and 1852. Two addi-

Fort Carroll: Located on a shoal four miles below Fort McHenry, its original construction was supervised by then Colonel Robert E. Lee.

tional conventions were held in 1860. The opposition also met in Baltimore City. In the evolution of political parties from National Republican to Wig to Constitutional Union, the city saw Henry Clay nominated in 1831, War of 1812 veteran General Winfield Scott in 1852, and John Bell in 1860. In 1860 the now powerful and fully developed Republican Party nominated Abraham Lincoln at its convention in Chicago.[4]

Known as the Monumental City, Baltimore could have been called the Convention City as well. There were many reasons for this, both distinct and subtle. Transportation was a key factor. The same shipping lines, railroads and roads that brought goods in and out of the city carried delegates as well. The city also boasted an ample supply of hotels, inns, and meeting places to accommodate the rise in population. A third reason for choosing Baltimore was its proximity to the nation's capital. Conventions were held in May while Congress was still in session. Politicians and special couriers could easily travel between the two cities along the Washington Branch of the Baltimore and Ohio Railroad after it was opened in 1835.

Finally there was Baltimore's exact position between North and South. Located only 30 miles below the Mason-Dixon Line, the city combined its Northern business affiliations with a distinct Southern society to create a "Free Zone" for political debate that may not have been possible had abolitionists traveled into the Deep South or slave owners to New England. This steady diet of conventions kept Baltimoreans

3

(D.C.T.)

Barnum's Hotel: Baltimore was the home of the Democratic National Convention between 1832 and 1852. One reason was its fine selection of hotels and meeting places.

politically active on issues ranging from national importance to the local ward level. The high level of energy exhibited on election day in Baltimore City led to a less flattering nickname — Mob Town, a carry-over from the political anti-federalist riot that maimed the venerated Revolutionary leader Richard Henry Lee on the streets of Baltimore in 1812.

The political campaign of 1860 marked the final steps toward disunion. The great debate was not between Lincoln and Douglas, but within the Democratic Party itself. The issue was Popular Sovereignty. Would new states be admitted to the Union as slave or free. Fearing that Douglas was against the expansion of slavery,

(D.C.T.)

Reverdy Johnson: Stephen A. Douglas stayed at his home during the convention of 1860. A brilliant lawyer, Johnson would be the first defense attorney for Mary Surratt in 1865.

delegates from the Deep South withdrew from the Democratic Convention held in Charleston, South Carolina. In an attempt to save the party, a second convention was called for in Baltimore on June 18.[5]

As the city overflowed with delegates, newspapermen, and a mass of spectators, Stephen A. Douglas took up residence at the home of the eminent Baltimore attorney, Reverdy Johnson. Across the square that exhibited the 1814 Battle Monument his opposition made its headquarters at the Gilmor House. The square was filled with speech makers, rival bands, and excited crowds. Less than a year later they would be replaced by occupation troops from the North.

A second Democratic National Convention was held at the Front Street Theater, known as the site where "The Star-Spangled Banner" was first sung in public in 1814. Admission was supposed to be free but scalpers reportedly received two to five dollars per ticket — a considerable sum at the time. This was also the first on-line convention. A special telegraph line was run from the theater to a main telegraph office which in turn sent out regular dispatches to the entire country. On the first day rival delegates from both Arkansas and Delaware erupted in separate acts of physical violence over who would be seated at the convention. It took three days before the credentials committee could present its findings. On day four a portion of the floor collapsed and a recess had to be called while repairs were made.[6]

Every night Monument Square was packed with rival bands and speakers sparking mass meetings from both camps which gave the usually dignified area a circus-like atmosphere. On the fifth day Douglas appeared to be gaining control of the convention when Charles Russell announced that the Virginia delegation was withdrawing. Several other

5

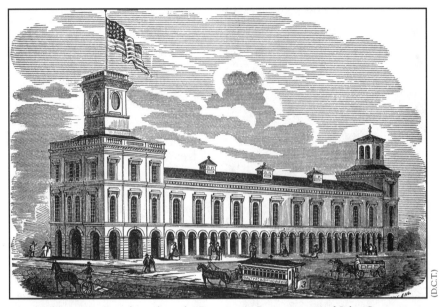

Maryland Institute: Dissidents from the Democratic Party nominated John C. Breckenridge here in 1860. In this same hall Presidents Franklin Pierce and Millard FIllmore were also nominated.

states followed suit including one-half the Maryland delegation. The dissidents met at the Maryland Institute Hall and held a third Democratic Convention. This time all the members were on the same page and John C. Breckenridge was nominated on the first ballot.[7]

Before the Democrats could complete their triathlon political event, a third national party took the stage in Baltimore. The Constitutional Union Party was founded by Senator John J. Crittenden of Kentucky in January of 1860. Its platform ignored the slavery issue and concentrated on preserving the Union. The party's national convention convened in Baltimore on May 9 at the Old First Presbyterian Church on the corner of North and Fayette Streets.[8]

The two leading candidates were John Bell of Tennessee and the venerable Sam Houston of Texas. After a short and, for the most part, harmonious convention John Bell was nominated for president and Edward Everett for vice-president. On the evening of May 14 a ratification meeting was held in Monument Square where a sixty-foot-long platform was erected complete with gas lights and patriotic banners. Maryland Senator Anthony Kennedy had the honor of introducing the candidates.[9]

When the election ended in November of 1860, Maryland voted decidedly against Lincoln. Breckenridge nudged Bell with 42,497 votes

The great debate during the presidential campaign of 1860 was within the Democratic Party. All three candidates were nominated in Baltimore City. Stephen A. Douglas (left) and John C. Breckenridge (right) split the party over the issue of Popular Sovereignty.

to 41,177. Douglas was a distant third with 5,873 while Lincoln received less than 2,300 votes statewide. With the Republicans solidly behind a single candidate, Abraham Lincoln became the 16th President of the United States.[10]

John Bell

Edward Everett

Senator John C. Crittenden founded
the Constitutional Union Party. Its
convention was held in Baltimore in
May of 1860 and nominated John
Bell for president and Edward
Everett for vice president.

John C. Crittenden

II

BALTIMORE AND THE SECESSION CRISIS OF 1861

*O*n December 17, 1860, the first secession convention of the year was held in Columbia, South Carolina. Decades of verbal warfare between North and South came to an end three days later when the convention unanimously passed an Ordnance of Secession taking South Carolina out of the Union. Other states in the Deep South rushed to hold their own conventions and one by one the stars began to fall out of Old Glory.[1]

The Virginia State Legislature slowed the pace of secession in the border states by calling for a Peace Conference in Washington, D.C. on February 4, 1861. The central theme of the conference was states rights. Although attended by representatives from twenty-one states, their recommendations were rejected by Congress on March 2 and the gulf between North and South widened yet again.[2]

As the border states debated their future positions in the Union, Abraham Lincoln began his journey to the White House. On the morning of February 11, 1861, the Wabash train moved out of Springfield, Illinois, and sped eastward carrying the 52-year-old President-elect. The journey to Washington took twelve days with whistle stops in seventy towns and cities. The highlight would be in Philadelphia, where on the 22nd at dawn, Lincoln would raise the nation's new 34 star flag over Independence Hall.

Before his departure for Harrisburg to address the State Legislature, Lincoln was introduced to Allan Pinkerton, a detective for the Philadelphia, Wilmington and Baltimore Railroad. Pinkerton's duty was to investigate suspicious activities in Baltimore concerning the destruction of railroad property.

The political excitement in Baltimore had become tense as citizens discussed the probability of war. Such shadows of discontent enabled Pinkerton to suspect a possible plot to harm the President-elect during his passage through Baltimore at noon on the 23rd. The plot, as later described by Pinkerton, was that unknown conspirators planned to ambush Lincoln's carriage during a prearranged disturbance as it made the half mile passage between the Calvert Street Station of the Northern Central to the Camden Street Station of the Baltimore and Ohio Railroad. Pinkerton emphasized that secrecy while traveling through Baltimore was an absolute necessity. The passage was all the more perilous since rail connections between the two stations necessitated the cars to be horse-drawn. A city ordinance prohibited the passage of engines through downtown because of the disruption to businesses along the waterfront district.

Pinkerton stressed the importance of postponing the scheduled trip to Harrisburg and moving immediately through Baltimore. That evening, Pinkerton's suspicions were strengthened by the arrival of Senator William Seward's son who carried a letter from his father warning of possible danger in Baltimore. Lincoln, nevertheless, kept his scheduled appointment in Harrisburg and agreed to an early rerouted passage through Baltimore via the Philadelphia, Wilmington and Baltimore Railroad.[3]

Allan Pinkerton: Founder of the most famous detective agency in the country. He convinced government officials that a plot existed in Baltimore to assassinate President-elect Lincoln as he passed through the city en route to his inauguration.

At 6 p.m., a special train consisting of a locomotive, tender and a single passenger car left Harrisburg for Philadelphia. At the same time telegraph lines to Baltimore were cut to prevent any unwarranted communications. Pinkerton joined the Lincoln party at 11 p.m. They secretly boarded a sleeping car that was attached to the train departing for Baltimore just before midnight. Arriving at the President Street Station at 3:30 a.m. the next morning, the car was hitched to a team of horses and pulled slowly along Pratt Street to the Camden Street Station on the west side of town. Within an hour it was coupled to a B&O train and en route to Washington. Once the President-elect had safely arrived, the wire service was reopened and Pinkerton sent a coded telegram to the president of the Philadelphia, Wilmington and Baltimore Railroad: "Plums delivered nuts safely." Translated the message read, "Pinkerton delivered President safely."[4]

At 12:30 p.m., the President-elect's scheduled train arrived from Harrisburg into the Calvert Street Station, one of the two depots of the Northern Central in Baltimore City. On board was Mrs. Lincoln, her three sons and John Hay, the President's private secretary. No less than 10,000 spectators waited for a glimpse of the new President. Needless to say the response was short of overwhelming, when they learned that Lincoln had bypassed their reception. Newspapers and cartoonists published the event accordingly.

As for the Lincoln family, in the interim hours before their scheduled departure from the Camden Station at 3 p.m., they were taken to the home of John S. Gittings the president of the Northern Central Railroad in the Mount Vernon district. Despite the raucous crowds that gathered outside, Mrs. Charlotte C.R. Gittings, a woman of pronounced Southern sentiments, entertained her husband's guests. This hand of hospitality in 1861 towards the Lincolns, would three years later, prove beneficial in a Presidential pardon for a friend, Samuel B. Hearn, who was sentenced to be executed at Fort McHenry in 1864.[5]

Many historians do not believe the plot ever existed. Pinkerton went on to provide bad information for the army field commanders during the war. Lincoln may well have come to regret the affair which embarrassed him nationally and did nothing to improve his relations with the state of Maryland.

O n February 18, the Maryland State Conference Convention met in Baltimore. This conference had no legal foundation and resulted in the division between the state legislators and Governor Thomas Holiday Hicks. The governor had been elected to office in 1858 as a member of the now defunct Know-Nothing Party. When he failed to consult with the legislature on matters concerning the impending national crisis, they revolted and held a mass meeting at the Maryland Institute Hall on February 1, at which time they condemned Hicks and called for an election of delegates to a state convention.

The Conference met only briefly. Realizing that Maryland would have no cause for secession if Virginia remained in the Union, delegates were sent to Richmond and the meeting adjourned. Before the Conference could take any substantial action, Governor Hicks finally called

Governor Thomas H. Hicks: Allowed the state to drift between Union and Secession until after most of the state legislature was arrested in September of 1861. He then came out in strong support of the Union.

a special session of the legislature. Its single accomplishment was to create a body that could have been converted into a secession convention had the circumstances been different.[6]

During the month of April 1861, events in Baltimore City as well as the nation as a whole moved quickly. At Chase's Wharf, Fells Point, the Richmond bark, *Fanny Crenshaw* was flying the Confederate flag, as hundreds looked on. On April 12, Confederate batteries ringing Charleston Harbor opened fire on Major Robert Anderson's command at Fort Sumter. The nation was at war! President Lincoln responded by calling for 75,000 volunteers to put down the rebellion. Two days later Virginia passed an Ordinance of Secession.

All eyes were now on Maryland. The only Southern state north of Washington, D.C., it separated the nation's capital from solid Union territory. Furthermore, through Baltimore ran Washington's only rail connection with the North courtesy of the Baltimore and Ohio Railroad.

On April 18, four companies of Pennsylvania militia left Harrisburg en route to Washington under the command of Major John C. Pemberton. They were accompanied by two companies of U.S. Artillery bound for Fort McHenry. When they arrived at Bolton Station, they were greeted by a hostile crowd that hurled oaths and bricks at them. Marshal George P. Kane utilized 130 officers of the Baltimore City Police Department to escort the Pennsylvania Volunteers to the B&O Station at Mount Clare. En route, Nickoles Biddle, a free colored man in the service of Captain James Wren, was struck in the head with a paving stone. The injury was not fatal and Biddle gained notoriety as the first casualty of the war.[7]

Throughout the 18th, Baltimore remained in an agitated state. Rival factions clashed in front of the newspaper offices when the latest bulletins were posted. Governor Hicks attempted to calm the storm by issu-

Nickoles Biddle: The colored servant of Captain James Wren, and member of the Washington Artillery of Pottsville, PA. He was struck in the head with a paving stone during their march through Baltimore in April of 1861 and thus awarded the title of first casualty of the war.

ing a statement that no Maryland troops would be sent out of the state other than to defend the nation's capital.

At this time the Palmetto flag of South Carolina was considered the ultimate emblem of secession. Wherever it appeared in the city it was quickly hauled down. Secession was a question not yet answered and this may explain why some chose to fly the National colors and others the state flag.[8]

On this same day a States Rights Convention was held in Taylor's Hall at Fayette and Calvert Streets. Ross Winans, the multi-millionaire industrialist who had built a railroad for the Tzar of Russia, pushed forth several resolutions condemning Lincoln's actions against the Southern states but falling short of advocating secession. This was one of the many moments during the month of April 1861 when the leading citizens of the state chose a reluctant position in the Union over outright secession. The next day would see the most chronicled event in the history of the city since the bombardment of Fort McHenry in 1814, and make Baltimore the first battlefield of the Civil War. This notion was put forth earlier by the *Baltimore American* "that Baltimore is to be the battlefield of the Southern Revolution." [9]

Following Lincoln's call for an army to suppress the rebellion, volunteers flocked to recruiting stations and independent militia companies collected themselves into regiments. Neither North nor South was prepared for instant mobilization and very few regiments possessed a full complement of men, uniforms, and equipment. The first to take the field fully armed and accompanied with a band was the Sixth Massachusetts Volunteer Regiment commanded by Colonel Edward F. Jones. Summoned to Washington to protect the capital, the regiment left

Boston on April 18 by train amidst patriotic allusions to the Minute Men who had fought at Lexington and Concord in April of 1775.[10]

In Philadelphia, Colonel Jones was informed by Samuel M. Felton, the man who had helped arrange Lincoln's train in February, that his passage through Baltimore might be opposed by Southern sympathizers. After crossing the Susquehanna River orders were given for the band to play only neutral tunes and the quartermaster issued 20 rounds of munitions to each man.[11]

The thirty-five car train arrived at the President Street Station on April 19 at 7 a.m. It carried not only the Sixth Massachusetts, but seven companies of unarmed Pennsylvania volunteers. Jones had planned to march his regiment en mass through the city. He ordered his men while en route to ignore verbal abuse, but if fired upon ".. take aim and be sure to drop him." For some reason the order was never given to unload the train and the cars were uncoupled and hitched to teams for the transit to Camden Station. As each successive car moved along Pratt Street more and more attention was drawn to the presence of the soldiers. Vocal abuse soon turned to violent action and the seventh car containing men from Company K was temporarily halted and received a good pelting of rocks and bottles interspersed with pistol shots. One soldier had his thumb shot off and three others were injured by missiles striking the glass windows. The eighth car in the procession was stopped at the intersection of Gay and Pratt Streets. A cart of sand was dumped on the tracks and anchors from the nearby docks placed across the rails. A pile of cobblestones slated for street repair was relocated to the improvised barricade. The next car had no chance of passing this point. The driver jumped out and hitched his team to the rear of the car making all possible speed back to the President Street Station. Four companies, about 200 men, were now cut off from the main force along with the band and Pennsylvania volunteers.[12]

Captain A.S. Follansbee, the senior officer, determined to press on to Camden Station on foot. A small detachment of Baltimore City policemen battled the crowd that now centered on the President Street Station as the soldiers formed up for the march.

No sooner had the march begun than a Southern patriot carrying a South Carolina flag placed himself in front of the soldiers causing them the insult of marching behind their enemy's banner and exciting the crowd to new heights. Pro-Union men soon joined the fracas and partly destroyed the Rebel flag before being overwhelmed by the opposition. The mob then began to stone the soldiers. At Fawn Street one man was knocked to the ground and set upon by the mob. Only the brave inter-

Captain A. S. Follansbee: Led five companies of the Sixth Massachusetts Regiment through the Pratt Street Riot.

vention by the Baltimore City police saved him from certain death. At Stiles Street two more men fell, but were able to regain their feet although they lost their muskets in the scuffle. Before he reached Pratt Street, Follansbee ordered the "double quick step," in an attempt to outdistance the mob. The soldiers pushed their way across the Jones Falls bridge which was partially blocked with workmen's tools and lumber abandoned by a repair crew.[13]

The first citizen known to have been shot was Francis X. Ward. The mob reacted by closing in on the soldiers in an attempt to grab their muskets. Two weapons were seized and one soldier killed.[14]

When Mayor Brown learned of the conflict on Pratt Street, he rushed to the scene and ordered Marshal Kane to bring as many policemen as possible to protect the soldiers. Traveling along Pratt Street he stopped at Smith's Wharf and ordered Sergeant McComas and his detail of four policemen to remove the anchors from the tracks there. He then pushed on and met the lost battalion just west of the Jones Falls bridge, shooting wildly over their shoulders and all the time being pelted with missiles of every description. The soldiers slowed their pace at the suggestion of Mayor Brown, but it did nothing to lessen the assault.

Unable to distinguish rioters from innocent bystanders, the soldiers fired in all directions. At the corner of South and Pratt Streets several citizens were seen to fall in one volley. Two blocks further west at Light Street, a soldier was mortally wounded and a boy on a ship in the harbor was killed by a stray bullet. At Light Street Mayor Brown left the column after making every effort to control the crowd and at great risk to himself of being shot. A boy in the crowd gave him a musket retrieved from a fallen soldier which erroneously gave rise to the story that he had shot one of the rioters.

The Riot: At Fawn Street a man was knocked to the ground and set upon by the mob.

(D.C.T.)

17

Mayor George W. Brown of Baltimore: Marched beside Captian Follansbee at the height of the riot in an attempt to stop the fighting. He was later arrested and confined at Fort McHenry.

By the time the soldiers had reached Charles Street four were dead and another three dozen wounded. Civilian casualties were also mounting. Some of the soldiers were cared for by blacks in a city who risked much in doing so. At this point Marshal Kane arrived with about 40 or 50 policemen. With drawn revolvers they formed a line behind the marching column and brought an end to the mob's pursuit. Follansbee's command soon reached Camden Street Station where a train of thirteen

George P. Kane: Marshal of the Baltimore City Police Department. Led a detachment of policemen which finally separated the soldiers from the rioters on Pratt Street. He was arrested when the army took control of the Police Department in June of 1861.

cars was waiting to take them out of the hostile city. The last civilian casualty of the day occurred about one half mile outside of the city. Mr. Robert Davis shook his fist at the train load of soldiers and was immediately shot dead from one of the cars. Word of his death rekindled the fire in the mob and they returned to President Street Station. The unarmed soldiers were at the mercy of the mob until a special train could return them to Philadelphia.[15] Baltimore was wild with fear and excitement in the aftermath of the riot. A popular misconception both in 1861 and today is that all Baltimoreans were of one mind — to attack any force representing the federal government and lead Maryland out of the Union as soon as possible. As noted in the previous narrative many citizens, both black and white, sought to aid the soldiers as did the Baltimore City Police Department as a whole. Mayor Brown, who was certainly in the eye of the storm for some time, stated after the war that "The mob, which was not very large ..." but that "the uproar was furious." A second witness, a Mr. C.W. Tailleure, was an editor for one of the local papers. In 1883 he wrote that there were no more than 250 to 500 people in the attacking mob at any one time. It may be presumed that a large number of citizens lined the streets and roof tops as spectators to such an unusual occurrence. However, a howling mob of even 500 people is not a fair representation of a city whose population exceeded 200,000.[16]

All this led to a great debate among the citizens as to what course of action the city should take. Governor Hicks called out the state militia to maintain law and order in Baltimore. Marshal Kane sent the following message to Bradley T. Johnson in Frederick City.

"Streets red with Maryland blood; send expresses over the mountains of Maryland and Virginia for riflemen to come without

19

William Ross: Member of the Baltimore City Police Department. Note large star badge on left side of coat. (Ninth-plate Ambrotype, ca 1860, from the collection of Ross J. Kelbaugh).

delay. Fresh hordes will be down on us to-morrow. We will fight them and whip them, or die."[17]

A mass meeting was held at Monument Square on the night of the riot. Governor Hicks, Mayor Brown, Severn T. Wallace, and others addressed the crowd. Governor Hicks spoke for the first time with any

At the corner of South and Pratt Streets several citizens were seen to fall in one volley.

(D.C.T.)

21

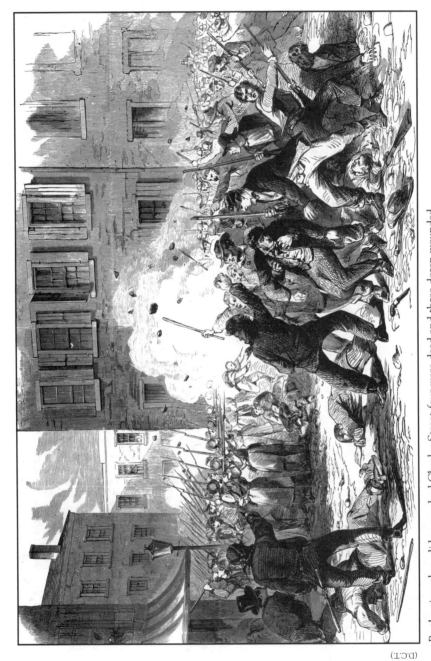

By the time the soliders reached Charles Street four were dead and three dozen wounded.

(D.C.T.)

22

conviction which, as events soon would show, would be short lived. "I am a Marylander; I love my State and I love the Union, but I will suffer my right arm to be torn from my body before I will raise it to strike a sister state." A telegram was sent to the President that same night signed by both Mayor Brown and Governor Hicks. "A collision between the citizens and the Northern troops has taken place in Baltimore and excitement is fearful. Send no more troops here."[18]

Later on that night, word reached Mayor Brown that more Union volunteers were en route by train from both Harrisburg and Philadelphia. If they attempted to pass through the city which was now packed with militiamen and armed civilians the loss of life and property would certainly be greater than the previous episode. A conference was held with the mayor and the Board of Police Commissioners and a decision was made to burn the railroad bridges north of Baltimore in order to prevent another conflict. A detachment of militia and city police were sent by special train to burn the bridges over the Gunpowder and Bush Rivers. Captain J.G. Johannes' company of the City Guard with a detachment of policemen and other volunteers burned the Northern Central bridges near Cockeysville. Governor Hicks returned to Annapolis the next day, leaving the mayor and city officials to suffer the consequences of their actions.[19]

On April 20, 1861, Baltimore entered into a period of "armed neutrality." The city council appropriated $500,000 for the defense of the city. Bank presidents Johns Hopkins, Columbus O'Donnell, and John Clark delivered the money to Mayor Brown. The national flag had now disappeared from view. A large Confederate flag flew from the States Rights headquarters on Fayette Street. The Minute Men, a pro-Union club on Baltimore Street replaced their U.S. Flag with a Maryland State flag. Baltimore was rapidly developing a siege mentality. Men and boys paraded around town wearing secession badges and volunteer companies from all over the state poured into the city. Ross Winans machine shops switched from producing locomotives to manufacturing pikes, musket balls, and an unusual steam powered machine gun.[20]

Defensive measures were also being taken at Fort McHenry. Fearing an attack by Rebels in Baltimore, the post commander, Captain John C. Robinson of the Fifth U.S. Infantry, ordered the magazine wall facing the city reinforced with timbers and sandbags. He also had gutters fabricated so that he could roll shells into the dry moat in case an attack came upon the walls. Finally, a field piece was sighted to cover the Fort Road coming from the city and a 10-inch columbiad, the fort's largest gun, positioned to fire on Monument Square, a distance of three miles.

Memories of the 19th of April were kept alive in the North with anti-Baltimore literature and stationery known as patriotic covers.

AUNER'S PRINTING OFFICE, EIGHTH AND MARKET.

THE
SLAIN AT BALTIMORE!

There's sorrow and there's weeping by mountain, vale and shore,
For Freedom's new slain martyrs,—*the Dead at Baltimore!*
There's a swelling cry for vengeance on those counterfeits of men,
Who haunt that hold of pirates,—that foul assassin's den.

And the hosts of truth are rising. From the giant woods of Maine
Come stalwart forms that fell her pines, 'mid winter's snow and rain;
From Hampshire, whose bare mountains as Freedom's altars swell,
Our Switzerland sends men as bold as Winkelried and Tell.

And from the fair Green Mountain State, come sons of those whose mark,
Once taught the foes of liberty to dread the name of Stark;
While first our Bay State soldiers swarm from workshop, store and mill,
As first they stood at Lexington, and first at Bunker Hill.

And brave Rhode Island, small but smart, sends warriors with her Sprague,
Whose coming foes shall learn to dread, as cities dread the plague:
And teachers of Connecticut their schools awhile dismiss,
To teach their foes a knowledge, whose "ignorance is bliss."

And lo! the Empire State is roused, from inland line to coast,
And from her thousand villages starts up an armed host;
While her Imperial City, through all its circles stirred,
Is as a trumpet through whose depths a nation's voice is heard.

And still, as in the days of old, New Jersey has her men,
And the hosts of war are swarming in the peaceful State of Penn;
And the solemn sound is rising, fast rising to a roar,
Like the voice of many waters,—*"the slain at Baltimore!"*

Hark! on the morning breezes, comes a low and threatening sound;
The mighty West is rising, and their marching shakes the ground;

As a countless herd of bisons over the level prairies rush,
Comes this eager host of warriors, to trample and to crush.

They have felt the Southron's insults, they have borne his bitter taunts,
They have listened without answer to his weak and childish vaunts;
Till the Nation's flag was trampled on, they patiently forebore,
But now they strike for Freedom—*and the slain at Baltimore!*

To a man the North has risen, and the Southrons shall be taught,
The weakness of their idol god, their Baal, their Juggernaut.
On his car they sit at leisure, and would have our freemen strip,
And drag it to the cracking of an overseer's whip.

They scorn our Northern workman, and his handicraft deride;
For their only skill is insolence, their capital is pride,
And what is old Virginia, with her boast of ancient stock,
But a beggar, by young children fed, from off the auction block?

And South Carolina chivalry is but a standing jest,
Her bravery, the rope, the chain, the pistol at the breast.
The other rebel States, more base, are reckless all of life,
For duels there are arguments, the readiest word a knife.

Then up and at them, freemen! the sword of justice draw!
And teach to all the lawless, the dignity of law;
Bid them learn that 'tis the peaceful who in war are truly great,
And that every rebel leader shall meet a traitor's fate.

And when the sound of conflict in speedy peace is hushed;
When the rebel ranks are scattered and their dark ambition crushed;
When the Union stands untarnished, as it stood in days of yore,
In our triumph we'll remember *the slain at Baltimore!*

C. S. S.

A. W. AUNER, SONG PUBLISHER, N. W. Cor. 8th and Market Sts., Philadelphia.

Secession Badge showing snake coiled around two Confederate Flags:
Men and boys paraded around town wearing secession badges.

On the night of April 20, Police Commissioner John W. Davis was sent to Fort McHenry by Charles Howard to warn Captain Robinson of a possible attack and offered to send a force of 200 men from the Maryland Guard to intercept the strike force. Captain Robinson informed the police commissioner that the Maryland Guard was not welcome at the fort and that if they ventured past the Catholic chapel on the Fort Road, a 1/4 mile away, he would open fire on them. One of the junior officers at the fort, lacking diplomacy in a time of crisis, threatened to fire on the Washington Monument which was located in the Mount Vernon district a known hotbed of Southern sympathizers. Mr. Davis responded: "If you do that, and if a woman or child is killed, there will be nothing left of you but your brass buttons to tell who you were."[21]

The next crisis came on April 21, when a force of over 1,000 Pennsylvania Volunteers moved from Harrisburg on the Northern Central and were stopped by the damaged bridge at Ashland. J. Morrison Harris, former member of the U.S. House of Representatives, entered the city from his home in Baltimore County and "...found a terrible condition of excitement." Fearing the next clash of arms would push Maryland out of the Union, he secured a special train from the always cooperative President Garrett of the Baltimore and Ohio Railroad and hastened to Washington in company with Senator Anthony Kennedy for an emergency meeting with President Lincoln. They also met with General Scott and Secretary of War Simon Cameron. All agreed to recall the Pennsylvania troops and sent General Howard with them on a return mission to seek out the Union field com-

Fort McHenry: Early view from a patriotic cover.

mander and have him withdraw the troops back across the state line. This was accomplished the next morning.[22]

Also on the 21st, Charles Howard consolidated all military companies and armed civilians in the city under the command of Isaac Ridgeway Trimble, a West Point graduate and an engineer. He would serve in the Confederate army, rising to the rank of Major General, and lose a leg in Picket's Charge at Gettysburg. This force acted on orders from the Police Commissioners, building barricades and doing guard duty as needed. On April 22, The [Baltimore] Sun paper reported: "300 to 400 of our most respected colored residents made a tender of their services to the city authorities …"[23]

Finally on April 22, Governor Hicks agreed to call the State Legislature into a special session. With Annapolis now in the hands of the Union army he choose Frederick City as the site. The Legislature convened on April 26. The next day the Senate unanimously voted on a declaration that stated it had no constitutional authority to consider the subject of secession. The House of Delegates concurred with a vote of 53 to 12.[24]

This was the last free act by that legislative body during the war. It did demonstrate that once removed from the hostile elements in Baltimore, the desire, statewide, was to preserve the Union and avoid the war if at all possible.

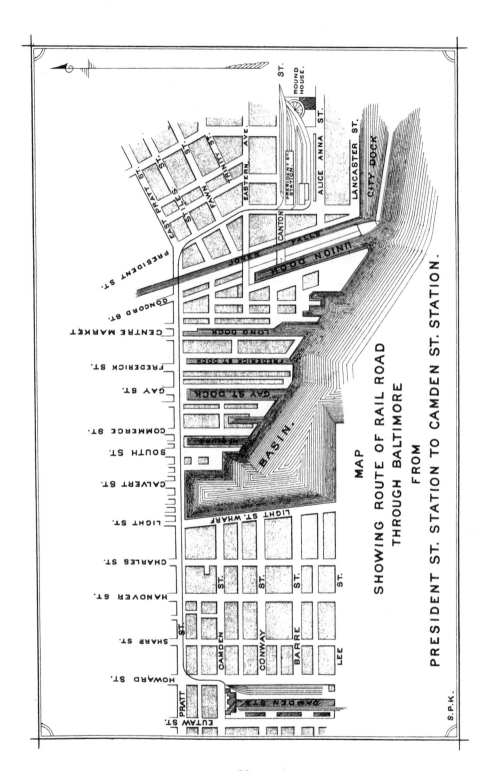

MAP

SHOWING ROUTE OF RAIL ROAD

THROUGH BALTIMORE

FROM

PRESIDENT ST. STATION TO CAMDEN ST. STATION.

28

III

THE OCCUPATION OF BALTIMORE

When the war began in April of 1861 there were no federal soldiers or fortifications in Baltimore City other than Fort McHenry. Following the attack on the Sixth Massachusetts Regiment, all Union troops were rerouted through Annapolis. Brigadier General Benjamin Butler was rewarded for his occupation of the state's capital by being appointed to command the Department of Annapolis on April 27, 1861. This was the federal government's first attempt to control the state of Maryland and indicated just how vital the railroad was in linking the nation's capital with the North. The boundaries of his department ran for 20 miles on either side of the Annapolis and Elk Ridge Railroad to Annapolis Junction. From there it ran south with the same dimensions along the Washington Branch of the Baltimore and Ohio Railroad to Washington and north to Baltimore.[1]

Brig. Gen. Benjamin F. Butler: He was removed from command for occupying Baltimore without orders from General Scott.

On May 5, Butler occupied Relay, 8 miles southwest of Baltimore. This was perhaps the most important railroad station in the country in 1861. From Relay the Thomas Viaduct carried the B&O over the Patapsco River and south to Washington City. Running west the main branch of the railroad passed through Harpers Ferry and Cumberland on its way to Ohio. A short distance to the northeast lay Baltimore City with its factories, docks, and railroad connections to the north. Butler positioned his artillery on both sides of the bridge and protected the tracks in all directions with outposts and roving patrols.[2]

Acting on orders from the commander-in-chief, General Winfield Scott, Butler's objective was to stop the flow of military supplies and recruits from Baltimore to Harpers Ferry and provide a defense against Rebel incursion into Baltimore. Scott's orders were clear — stop all secessionist activities. To do so, Butler theorized he would need to stop it at its source. With Annapolis and Relay secured, Butler undertook a plan without Scott's knowledge to move forward and occupy Baltimore.

Towards evening on May 13, Butler loaded artillery and infantry onto a train that had a locomotive at each end. He then proceeded towards Frederick where the Maryland Legislature was scheduled to convene on the 17th. Two miles out of Relay he stopped the train. To avoid suspicion Butler ordered half the train to proceed to Frederick. The other half to Baltimore. Arriving near sundown 1,000 soldiers consisting of the Sixth Massachusetts Regiment and the Boston Light Artillery disembarked at the Camden Street Station. Under the cover of a thunderstorm, Butler moved quickly to occupy Federal Hill, and sent the following message to the commander of Fort McHenry; "I have taken possession of Baltimore. My troops are on Federal Hill, which I can hold with the aid of my artillery. If I am attacked to-night, please open upon [Battle] Monument Square with your mortars."[3]

The next morning, the citizens of Baltimore awoke to find a fortified Union encampment with the stars and stripes waving defiantly upon the hill. Overnight armed resistance in the city came to an end. One person who was on the scene and wrote about it in his memoirs after the war was McHenry Howard. High in the social order of Baltimore, he was the grandson of both Revolutionary War General John Edgar Howard and Francis Scott Key. Howard was a member of the Maryland Guard, a battalion of state militia formed after John Brown's raid in 1859. The battalion was put on a high state of alert following the Pratt Street Riot. On the night of May 13, they were ordered to report to the armory at Carroll Hall.

"We found the place dimly lighted and the guns being carried off, singly and by twos and threes or more, by any members of the

Union Artillery guarding the Thomas Viaduct: Relay was perhaps the most important railroad station in the country in 1861.

Battalion who would undertake to hide them. The reason was that General Butler had occupied, or was about occupying, Federal Hill with an overwhelming force and the city would certainly fall into his hands in the morning. I took and carried home three muskets, but did not attempt to hide them specially, for I apprehended that my father [Charles Howard] would be arrested, as President of the Board of Police, and his house, on Cathedral Street next to Emmanuel Church, would be searched, and it would not be well to have any concealed arms discovered there. These were found and seized when he was arrested afterwards, [and sent to Fort McHenry], but I believe very few others were ever found, although diligently sought for. Many were taken South and did good service there, while some, no doubt, remain hidden away and forgotten to this day. The Armory was stripped by one or two o'clock .... The next morning not a uniform was seen on the streets of which they had made so picturesque before, and General Butler took possession of the city. I saw him as he dismounted to establish his headquarters at the Gilmor House on Monument Square, and I walked over to Federal Hill and looked at the troops fixing their camps on that commanding eminence."

*I*n the days that followed many members of the Maryland Guard went south with their weapons and equipment from the armory. Howard left the city on June 1, after he was informed by Severn Teakle Wallis that no organized resistance would take place in Maryland. Four years later on April 17, 1865, he and his brother marched past their parents home as prisoners of war in route to the federal prison at Johnson's Island, Ohio.[4]

On May 14, Butler issued a "Proclamation to the Citizens of Baltimore," stating that he had "occupied the city for the purpose, among other things, of enforcing respect and obedience to the laws, as well as the state ..." On learning of the proclamation, Winfield Scott ordered Butler to issue "no more proclamations" and stressed that Butler's "hazardous occupation of Baltimore was made without my knowledge ... It is a God-send that it was without conflict of arms." On May 15, Butler was relieved of command and ordered to Fort Monroe, guarding the strategic harbor of Hampton Roads, Virginia.[5]

In the years to follow, Butler became infamous in the South as the military governor of Louisiana and proved to be an inept field commander. Ironically the fact that he almost single-handedly saved the state of

Maryland for the Union has been largely overlooked by historians. His occupation of Annapolis brought protection to the Naval Academy and prevented the state capital from becoming a power base for secessionists. By seizing the Annapolis and Elk Ridge Railroad he reopened communication with Washington which at that time greatly feared an attack by combined Maryland and Virginia forces. His occupation of Relay secured a vital section of the Baltimore and Ohio Railroad. It also placed him in an excellent position to stem the flow of supplies and recruits from Baltimore to the rapidly forming Confederate army at Harpers Ferry. Last but not least, Butler took Baltimore City out of the war as far as the Confederacy was concerned, strengthened the hand of Union men in the state, and perhaps transferred the opening battle lines of the Civil War from the Susquehanna to the Potomac River.

He was replaced by Major General George Cadwalader who arrived with three Pennsylvania regiments from Philadelphia. Camp Cadwalader, located in Locust Point, consisted of the Second Philadelphia National Guard, the Third Philadelphia Light Guards and the First Pennsylvania Regiment, whose 360 tents fronted the Fort Road from Fort McHenry to Federal Hill.[6]

A veteran of the Mexican War, for which he received a brevet promotion of major general, Cadwalader's appointment would soon cast him to center stage of national politics. On May 16 he received the following orders from General Winfield Scott, via the President: "Herewith you will receive a power to arrest persons under certain circumstances and to hold them prisoners though they should be demanded by writs of habeas corpus. This is a high and delicate trust and as you cannot fail to perceive to be executed with judgment and discretion..." For Marylanders and the nation, the President's suspension of the writ of habeas corpus would soon raise Constitutional issues and spark controversy at the gates of Fort McHenry.[7]

On May 17, 1861, with opposition to federal law within Maryland, Lincoln ordered the suspension of the writ of habeas corpus along the military railroad line between Philadelphia, Washington and Annapolis. With this suspension the President gave de facto powers to the United States Army to place under arrest spies and Confederate sympathizers whose acts and statements were inimical to the U.S. Government. Those arrested were placed under the authority of the State Department and detained at various military posts, among them Fort McHenry. It would not be until February 14, 1862, that these prisoners would be transferred to the War Department.[8]

Determined to keep Maryland within the Union, Lincoln had extended his Constitutional authority without consent of Congress. Until

Federal Hill: From Relay Butler moved a thousand men by special train to Baltimore on the night of May 13, 1861.

34

Congress could convene in July, Lincoln was determined to preserve his tenuous hold on Maryland, thus safeguarding the capital of the United States.

The writ of habeas corpus predates our own Constitution to English common law of the English *Magna Carta*. In brief, it states that a citizen being arrested must be charged with a specific crime or they cannot be imprisoned. It is a safeguard against unlawful seizures and violation of due process.[9]

On the morning of May 25, John Merryman, a known Southern sympathizer and first lieutenant of the Baltimore County Horse Guards, was arrested at his estate north of Baltimore, "Hayfields," in Cockeysville. Taken to Fort McHenry, Merryman was confined for treason and aiding the enemy by burning bridges of the Northern Central Railroad in Baltimore County on the night of April 22, 1861. Merryman had acted under orders of city officials.[10]

With the arrest of Merryman, Lincoln's decision to suspend the writ resulted in a conflict between the executive and judicial powers of the government. Lincoln's administration was about to be tested by the intervention of the eighty-four year old Chief Justice Roger Brooke Taney. Arrested without a warrant and held without formal charges, Merryman was denied permission to have legal counsel. A petition was therefore prepared on his behalf and taken to Justice Taney. The petition requested that a writ of habeas corpus be issued to the fort's commander, Major George Cadwalader, for Merryman's release. From the Old Masonic Hall on St. Paul Street, Taney sent a writ to Cadwalader to show just cause for Merryman's detention and demanded his release since no specific charges had been presented. Cadwalader ignored the writ and refused to attend a hearing on May 27, informing the U.S. District Court by messenger he would detain Merryman citing Presidential orders.[11]

Taney, in response, ordered an attachment to the writ to be served on Cadwalader. However, the U.S. Marshal delivering the writ the next day was refused entry at the fort's outer gate. Informed of the refusal Taney, rather than risk a confrontation, sent his opinion to the President on June 2. His now famous Ex-Parte Merryman decision ruled that the President, under the Constitution and laws of the United States, "cannot suspend the privilege of the writ of habeas corpus, nor authorize any military officer to do so. Only Congress has that power."[12]

Taney sent his opinion so that the President could adhere to his Constitutional oath of office. Lincoln ignored the writ. In a message to a special session of Congress on July 4, Lincoln stated in his only known referral to the case, "To state the question more directly, are all the laws, but one, to go unexecuted, and the government itself go to pieces, lest that one be violated."[13]

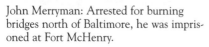

John Merryman: Arrested for burning bridges north of Baltimore, he was imprisoned at Fort McHenry.

Roger Brook Taney: This Maryland born Chief Justice of the Supreme Court rendered the Dred Scott Decision. His defense of John Merryman led to Lincoln's suspension of the writ of habeas corpus.

Lincoln's refusal revealed the federal government's determination to halt any secession movement in Maryland. With the support of the military, Lincoln expanded the arrest of suspected citizens to other states. In brief, the President had collected unto himself, with Congress in recess, the legislative, judicial and executive powers of government, in the belief he was upholding his oath of office to preserve the Union, since one-third of the states had seceded. It would be two years before Congress officially authorized the suspension of the writ of habeas corpus as a special wartime act granted to the President on March 3, 1863.[14]

In the weeks that followed, political arrests were common as military officials continued to tighten their hold on Baltimore and the state. Major General Nathaniel P. Banks replaced General Cadwalader as Department Commander between June 23 and July 21. Like Butler, he too was a politically appointed general from Massachusetts having served as Speaker of the House of Representatives before being elected as Governor of the state in 1858. Acting on orders from General Winfield

Scott he arrested Marshal George Kane on June 27. In a proclamation to the citizens of Baltimore on the same day he stated that the Police Marshal was considered an enemy of the federal government.

"Under such circumstances the Government cannot regard him otherwise than as the head of an armed force hostile to its authority and acting in concert with its avowed enemies."

Colonel John R. Kenly of the First Maryland Volunteers was made acting provost marshal. At 4:00 a.m. on the morning of July 1, Banks sent a detachment of Pennsylvania soldiers to arrest the four Baltimore City Police Commissioners and take them to Fort McHenry. They were Charles Howard, president; John W. Davis, Charles P. Hicks, and William H. Gatchell.[15]

On July 25, Merryman was allowed to return home. His release from Fort McHenry most likely resulted from a conversation between the

The arrest of Marshal Kane from the front cover of the July 6, 1861 edition of *Leslie's Illustrated Newspaper*.

(D.C.T.)

Maj. Gen. Nathaniel P. Banks:
Commanded the Department of
Annapolis for less than two months.
During this time he arrested the Police
Marshal of Baltimore City.

commander of Fort McHenry and Secretary of War Simon Cameron at
the fort on July 4. Regardless of Maryland's position in the Union,
Baltimore was the first occupied city in the South during the Civil War.[16]

IV

THE WAR YEARS

*B*utler had taken Baltimore out of the war as far as the South was concerned, but no one could take the South out of Baltimore. James Ryder Randall was teaching school in Louisiana when he read an account of the street fighting in Baltimore on the 19th of April. The report disclosed the fact that his close personal friend and college roommate from Georgetown, Francis X. Ward, had been mortally wounded. That night, unable to sleep, he transferred his shock and grief into a nine-stanza poem which he entitled "My Maryland." The next day he read the poem to his literature class at Poydras College. The students urged him to have it published and he submitted it to the *New Orleans Delta*. "My Maryland" first appeared in print on April 26. It was widely reprinted throughout the Southern states and reached Baltimore in late May where it was published by *The South* on the last day of the month.[1]

By June the sentiments of the poem were outlawed in Baltimore, but it continued to circulate secretly among Southern sympathizers. Attempts were made to put the words to music but the efforts fell short until two sisters, Jennie and Hettie Cary, changed the refrain to "Maryland, My Maryland." They sent to have it set to the music of the Yale college song, "Lauriger Horitis." A friend of the Cary sisters, Rebecca Lloyd Nicholson, arranged to have the song printed in sheet music. Forty-seven years earlier in 1814, her grandfather, Joseph H. Nicholson (brother-in-law of Francis Scott Key), had arranged another song to be published, "The Star-Spangled Banner." The almost finished product was then sent to the publishers, Miller and Beacham, to be made into sheet music. Charles Ellerbrock, an employee of the company, substituted the melody from "Tannenbaum, O Tannenbaum" before it actually went to press.

This collaboration resulted in one of the most popular songs of the war. Illegal in Maryland, due to the federal crack down, it was proudly sung on both sides of the Potomac River. In July 1861, the Cary sisters and friends sang the song at the headquarters of General Pierre Beauregard at Fairfax County Courthouse in Virginia. In September 1862, soldiers of the Army of Northern Virginia sang it as they crossed the river into Maryland.

Reflecting the danger of the time, the author's name does not appear on wartime copies of the sheet music. Instead the title page reads, "Written by a Baltimorean in Louisiana." In 1939, the Maryland General Assembly made "Maryland, My Maryland" the official state song. Just like "The Star-Spangled Banner," it has received criticism from time to time, but like our National Anthem, it was written in a single night as the result of a great historical event — one for the state and one for the nation, both in Baltimore.[2]

*P*erhaps no other prisoner, citizen or soldier who was held at Fort McHenry was more flamboyant than that of "the French Lady," who was involved in one of the most daring naval captures of the war. The affair involved the capture of the federal bay steamer *St. Nicholas* a 1,200 ton passenger-freight side-wheeler running the Chesapeake between Baltimore and Georgetown, Maryland, on the Potomac.

Richard Thomas, born in St. Mary's County on October 23, 1833, was the son of a former speaker of the House of Delegates and nephew of an ex-governor of Maryland. Thomas briefly attended the U.S. Military Academy in 1850. Leaving the academy, he traveled to the Far East to fight Chinese pirates, then to Italy where he joined, as a soldier of fortune, Garibaldi's national liberation army. Here, it seems, he earned the name "Zarvona." Returning home, he outlined his plan to capture the U.S. Warship *Pawnee* to Virginia Governor Letcher, who with others, lent support for the venture. Thomas now focused his efforts towards the *St. Nicholas*, his instrument to carry out the plan.

The *St. Nicholas* frequently supplied the *Pawnee* which patrolled the southern Chesapeake for Confederate blockade runners from the Eastern Shore. On the afternoon of June 28, 1861, the *St. Nicholas* left Baltimore on a routine trip for Southern Maryland. Among those who booked passage was a "French Lady" of dark complexion and rather masculine features. During the passage, it was reported the lady tossed her fan about at various officials and conversed quite fluently in French. When the *St. Nicholas* stopped briefly at Point Lookout, Maryland, to pick up passengers, the lady excused herself from her admirers and returned to her stateroom.

In the early morning hours of the 29th, the *St. Nicholas* steered up the Potomac River for Georgetown while the Point Lookout passengers lounged about on deck. The lady soon reappeared on deck as her true self — Colonel Richard Thomas, of the Confederate Potomac Zouaves — armed with a cutlass and revolver. Orders were quickly issued to his compatriots and the capture of the *St. Nicholas* took only moments — much to the surprise of the ship's officers. A fellow Marylander and compatriot, Captain Nicholas Hollins, took command.

With the successful capture of the *St. Nicholas*, Thomas directed her to the Virginia shore at Coan River to discharge unwilling passengers and take aboard additional Confederate volunteers. The original plan to capture the *Pawnee* was abandoned when it was learned she unexpectedly had to return to Washington.

The *St. Nicholas* proceeded for Fredericksburg capturing three vessels laden with valuable freight. With her prizes in tow, the *St. Nicholas* arrived, where Thomas's Potomac Zouaves were royally received by the Governor.[3]

In Baltimore, the piracy of the *St. Nicholas* embarrassed federal officials who moved quickly to capture Thomas. On July 9, Provost Marshal John R. Kenly, ordered the steamer *Chester* in pursuit, her crew augmented with soldiers from Fort McHenry. Even as the *Chester* departed, two Baltimore policemen were already in Anne Arundel County in an unrelated arrest. Returning to Baltimore on board the steamer *Mary Washington* the policemen learned of Thomas's presence on board, who was returning to Baltimore to repeat his venture. The police ordered the *Mary Washington* to Fort McHenry's dock instead of proceeding to the city. Thomas in disguise, grew suspicious and according to accounts, a dramatic confrontation ensued resulting in Thomas's capture. He was quickly taken to the fort and indicted on charges of piracy and treason and "confined with seven other equally desperate" companions by orders of General Nathaniel Banks, commander of the Department of Annapolis. Among Thomas's personal effects was a commission dated July 1, 1861, as colonel in the Virginia volunteer forces.

In a War Department report two months later, Major General John Dix described his celebrated State Department prisoner as "rich, intelligent and resolute. His nervous system is much broken by confinement and want of active occupation." Thomas was denied parole or even permission to leave his cell for exercise.

On December 2, nearly six months after his capture, Thomas was transferred to Fort Lafayette in New York harbor. The case prompted the attention of the War and State Departments and even the President. Witnesses for the prosecution were detained at Fort McHenry awaiting the trial that never materialized. The Governor of Virginia protested Thomas's imprisonment and threatened to execute several federal officers held as hostages if any harm came to Thomas.

In April 1863, after nearly two years imprisonment, under an exchange authorized by Secretary of War Edwin M. Stanton, Thomas was released and immediately left for Paris, France. With Thomas's departure, the detained witnesses were released and the case of "Zarvona — The French Lady Affair" came to an end. Unfortunately no known portrait survives of Colonel Richard Thomas nor of the "French Lady."[4]

*I*n July, Major General John A. Dix took command of what would eventually be called the Middle Department. The geographic area of his department was the states of New Jersey and Pennsylvania, the Eastern Shore counties of Maryland and Virginia, and the Maryland counties of Cecil, Harford, Baltimore, and Anne Arundel with headquarters in Baltimore City. He arrived just three days after the first great battle of the war, in Manassas, Virginia. When news arrived of the defeat of the Union army on July 21 it carried hopes for the secessionists in Baltimore who "were ripe for revolt." Confederate colors were prominently displayed throughout the city while rumors strengthened Southern hopes that a Rebel force would advance and liberate Maryland.[5]

Determined to secure Baltimore and Fort McHenry from any bold Southern coup de main, Dix strengthened the federal government's hold on Baltimore and forbade the display of Confederate colors. A series of fortifications and redoubts were begun to guard the city's main avenues and rail lines, in effect, surrounding Baltimore with federal troops. Only by a display of military activity did Dix succeed in averting any bloodshed like that which had shown itself on April 19.

Shortly after taking command, Dix, in a genuine display of gentlemanly tactfulness, entertained several prominent ladies of Southern persuasion at Fort McHenry. It was reported that following an afternoon

Maj. Gen. John A. Dix: First Commander of the Middle Department.

reception on the piazza of his quarters, Dix invited his guests to walk along the walls of the fort. At one point, according to his son who published his memoirs, he stopped at one of the two Columbiads and commented:

> "Ladies there will be no more trouble in the city unless it is created by persons of your own social position; the common people will not rise until they see the aristocracy of Baltimore moving. The safety of the town and the lives of its citizens are therefore, substantially in your hands. Will you oblige me by mounting these steps, looking over the top of that gun, and noting the place to which it points. "It points to Monument Square!" "Yes," replied the General, "and I now tell you that if there should be another uprising in Baltimore, I shall be compelled to try to put it down; and that gun is the first that I shall fire."[6]

Needless to say, Dix had made his intended impression on the Southern ladies.

Following the Confederate victory at Manassas, Virginia, federal officials were fearful that the Maryland Legislature would withdraw the state from the Union. With this in mind, they took measures to arrest suspected members assembling in Frederick, Maryland, before a feared vote of secession on September 17. On the 11th, Secretary of War Simon Cameron issued the following order to General Nathaniel Banks:

> "General: The passage of any act of secession by the Legislature of Maryland must be prevented. If necessary, all or any part of the members must be arrested. Exercise your own judgment as to the time and manner, but do the work efficiently."[7]

Banks immediately put the order into action. A midnight raid under the direction of Alan Pinkerton, who headed the Union spy network, netted thirty-one members of the legislature as well as other prominent sympathizers. Included among these were the Mayor of Baltimore, George W. Brown, and the editors of two newspapers, William W. Glenn of *The Exchange* and Thomas W. Hall of *The South*, both of whom were ordered to suspend their papers and sent to Fort McHenry.

The September arrests continued throughout the city. Lawrence Sangston, a member of the legislature, remembered being aroused from his home at midnight and informed he was to be taken to the Fort.

> "We proceeded to the Fort; met numerous carriages on the road and at the gates of the Fort, showing the arrests were extensive. On entering the Fort, was received by Col. [William] Morris, and ushered into an unfurnished room, where I found Messrs. [T. Parkin] Scott, [Severn T.] Wallis, [William G.] Harrison and [Henry] Warfield of the Legislature, Mr. May, of Congress ..."[8]

Governor Hicks, forgetting his speech at Monument Square on April 19, approved the arrests saying "We can no longer mince matters with these desperate people. I concur in all that you have done." General Dix, who temporarily commanded the fort commented that,

> "I do not think this is a suitable place for them ....It is too near the seat of war which may possibly be extended to us. It is also too near a great town, in which [there are] multitudes who sympathize with them, [and] who are constantly applying for interviews...."[9]

*T*he interviews by the press greatly annoyed federal authorities who viewed the disloyal Southern journals as "misrepresentations of the conduct and motives of the government, and the publications of intelligence that were calculated to aid and encourage the public enemy." The arrest of a particular Baltimore editor was not without irony. As the military parades and speeches in the city honored the forty-seventh anniversary of the Battle of Baltimore in 1814, military officials had also arrested Frank Key Howard, a co-editor of *The Exchange*. Mr. Howard's political activities were well known through his editorials. On September 13 at Fort McHenry, within this already regarded landmark of American history, an ironic twist of fate would intervene. Howard eloquently described his imprisonment at the fort. His words embodied the reflections of many Marylanders who were held at what became known as "An American Bastile." From his second story prison quarters within the fort, he wrote:

"When I looked out in the morning, I could not help being struck by an odd, and not so pleasant a coincidence. On that day, forty-seven years before on a British ship [actually an American flag-of-truce vessel], my grandfather had witnessed the bombardment of Fort McHenry. When on the following morning, the hostile fleet drew off, defeated, he wrote the song so popular throughout the country, "The Star-Spangled Banner." As I stood upon the very scene of that conflict, I could not but contrast my position with his, forty-seven years before. The flag which he so proudly hailed, I saw waving, at the same place, over the victims of as vulgar and brutal a despotism as modern times have witnessed."[10]

Sharing his quarters was Lawrence Sangston, a Baltimore delegate who recalled spending the afternoons at the fort "in pacing the portico reading and conversation with the other state prisoners ... and looking out upon a chicken-coop of a garrison..."

Another twist of fate was the arrest of George Armistead Appleton near the scene of the Battle of North Point in 1814 with a secession flag in his carpet bag. Mr. Appleton was the eighteen-year-old grandson of Lt. Colonel George Armistead who commanded Fort McHenry during the War of 1812.[11]

The thirty-one legislators and others who had been arrested and sent to Fort Warren in Boston harbor and Fort LaFayette in New York, were released following the Maryland elections on November 27, 1862, upon taking the oath of allegiance. In a report dated September 30, 1864, by a commission to examine the sixteen cases of prisoners of state held at Fort McHenry, the commissioners found that:

"...the papers in these cases was in many instances necessarily meager, many of the parties having been arrested in haste by officers on the march and upon representations made by the loyal people in disturbed districts, sufficiently justifying the officers who arrested them..."[12]

From the arrest of John Merryman on May 25 to December 30, 1861, one hundred and twelve citizens became prisoners of the State Department. By the war's end an estimated 2,200 civilians would be arrested and detained at Fort McHenry.[13]

Prior to the outbreak of the war, recruiting for soldiers to serve in the United States Army had gone very slowly in Baltimore. *The Baltimore American* reported on April 18, that less than twenty men had enlisted at the recruiting office on Camden Street. At the same time the state of South Carolina had been actively recruiting men from an office near Centre Market. During the months of February, March, and April, approximately 500 men were enlisted to serve in artillery units in Charleston harbor. After the occupation of Fort Sumter many of these men served there in Alfred Rhett's First Regular Heavy Artillery Battalion.[14]

Lincoln's first call for volunteers went unanswered in Maryland during the uncertain days of "armed neutrality." In May a second call was made for 42,000 men to serve for three years. Maryland lawyer, John Reese Kenly, a Mexican War veteran and Brigadier General in the Maryland Militia, opened a recruiting office at 112 Baltimore Street on May 6. One month later Kenly took command of the First Maryland Infantry Regiment at Camp Carroll, having been appointed colonel on June 11 by the President. In a grand ceremony on June 18, the regiment received its flag from a group of patriotic ladies from West Baltimore. Each regiment during the Civil War carried a state and national flag referred to as its colors. The flags were the heart of the regiment and were often presented by special committees or supporters of the unit. With the regiment drawn up in front of the Carroll Mansion, a procession of thirty-four young ladies in white dresses, one for each star in the flag, passed between the two lines of soldiers as a Pennsylvania band played patriotic airs. Miss Emma Lawrenson had the honor of presenting the flag to Colonel Kenly. After a brief acceptance speech, Kenly presented Miss Lawrenson with a wreath of flowers and then all the ladies sang "The Star-Spangled Banner."[15]

Life in Baltimore was continuously influenced by the presence of the military in the city. On September 4, General Dix issued an order prohibiting the display or sale of secession badges, flags, pictures, song sheets, photographs, neckties, infants' socks, or any other emblem of the

Confederacy. Such a trifling offense as a child wearing red and white stockings could initiate an arrest by the provost marshal. Dix did back away from the slave issue. "Do not interfere in any manner with persons held in servitude."[16]

The state elections of 1861 were held on November 6. It was the first of many influenced by the federal government in Maryland during the war. Federal soldiers were stationed at polling places throughout the state. Pro-Southern voters were intimidated or arrested on trumped up charges. Massachusetts soldiers bragged about voting the Union Ticket in Baltimore. Augustus W. Bradford defeated the Democratic candidate General Benjamin C. Howard to become Maryland's second wartime governor.[17]

(D.C.T.)

John R. Kenly: Recruited the first Maryland Union regiment to take the field. Later he commanded the Maryland Brigade.

1862

*T*hroughout the spring and summer of 1862 Confederate forces in Virginia defeated one Union army after another. In the Shenandoah Valley, General Thomas J. "Stonewall" Jackson out marched the army of General Nathaniel P. Banks and launched a surprise attack to cut him off at Front Royal on May 23. The only force to oppose this move was the First Maryland Regiment supported by four companies of Pennsylvania and New York troops and two guns of Knapp's Battery. Kenly fought a stubborn rear guard action that bought Banks the time he needed to retreat down the valley. By the end of the day most of the men in the First Maryland had been killed or captured. Leading the attack on the Confederate side was Colonel Bradley T. Johnson and the First Maryland Infantry, C.S.A. Kenly was wounded and taken prisoner near the end of the day.[18]

Patriotic Stationery: Top: Pro-Secession envelope outlawed by General Dix in 1861. Bottom: Pro-Union envelope, represents a different point of view.

When word of Banks' defeat reached Baltimore, Kenly was erroneously reported to have been killed. Gangs of Union men took to the streets threatening and beating known Southern sympathizers. Mr. Bolivar D. Daniels would have been hung if it were not for the intervention of the Baltimore City Police.[19]

The unrest lasted for two days. On Monday the 20th of May, a mob attacked the maintenance shops at Mount Clare. On Tuesday, a large crowd formed in front of the pro-Union paper *The Baltimore American* and from there proceeded to visit several known Southern establishments including the *Maryland News Sheet,* the Maryland Institute, the Holliday Street Theater, and the Maryland Club. All were threatened with violence if they did not display an American flag.[20]

In June, Major General John E. Wool took command of the Middle Department. Born in 1789, he was the oldest general officer in either army, having served in the War of 1812, and one of only four general officers in the Regular Army when the war began. Wool laid a heavy hand on the civilian population in Baltimore. Immediately after he took command he denounced both Governors Hicks and Bradford for not supporting the Union cause and launched a new series of indiscriminate arrests, that took their toll on Loyalists as well as Secessionists.[21]

In late July a number of Union men held a meeting in Baltimore and formed a special committee to investigate corruption and disloyalty within the city government. When the committee presented its findings on October 28, General Wool had his soldiers raid the meeting. The evidence was confiscated and the committee members, including Colonel Thomas R. Rich, aid-de-camp to Governor Bradford, hustled through the streets of Baltimore to a waiting steamer at Light Street Wharf and shipped off to Fort Delaware. Governor Bradford wrote in protest to President Lincoln, "Our whole loyal community regards this as the grossest outrage and demands their release."

Wool also hit at Southern sympathizers. He arrested Charles H. Kerr for composing the "Stonewall Quickstep" and Henry McCaffrey for publishing the sheet music, both were removed to Fort McHenry. The almost unanimous unpopularity of General Wool caused his removal in December of 1862.[22]

Defeat followed defeat for the federal armies in Virginia. General George B. McClellan led his Army of the Potomac to the outskirts of Richmond before being turned back by the builder of Fort Carroll, Major General Robert E. Lee. General Pope was also defeated at the Second Battle of Bull Run in August. Lee was now determined to invade the North. A victory in federal territory might bring European recognition to the young Confederate States of America. Given the chance, it was thought that Maryland would still leave the Union or at the very least

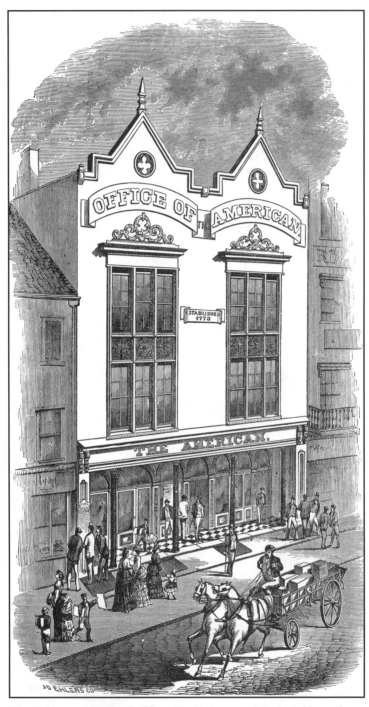

The Baltimore *American* Building: Pro-Union crowds gathered here after Colonel Kenly was reported killed at the battle of Front Royal.

yield thousands of recruits for his army. While Lee crossed the Potomac River and occupied Frederick, Maryland, during the first week of September, the wreckage of two Union armies milled about the federal capital. On September 2, President Lincoln reluctantly gave McClellan a second chance to command the Army of the Potomac.

With the first Confederate invasion under way, panic set in in Baltimore, Washington, and the major cities in Pennsylvania. The size and direction of Lee's army was unknown. Baltimore was presumed to be a target. Fortunately a new military force was stationed in Baltimore. The Maryland Brigade, consisting of five infantry regiments and a battery of artillery

(D.C.T.)

Maj. Gen. John E. Wool: Oldest general officer in either army.

had just been organized under the newly appointed Brigadier General John R. Kenly. On September 7, Kenly was given command of all troops in Baltimore other than those stationed in the forts. He moved his old First Regiment into the city and made his headquarters at the Eutaw House.[23]

On September 17, 1862, the Battle of Antietam was fought near the Washington County town of Sharpsburg. Lee's invasion was turned back and Maryland remained in the Union. A tactical draw, Lincoln quickly declared it a victory and issued the Emancipation Proclamation freeing all slaves held within any state "...in rebellion against the United States..." Because Maryland had not seceded from the Union, slavery remained a legal institution until abolished by the state constitution of 1864.[24]

The battlefield laid 75 miles away from Baltimore, yet, the thunderous sound of field ordnance echoing on the landscape was heard by Dr. Myron Robinson, Assistant Hospital Surgeon, Second U.S. Artillery at Fort McHenry. In a letter home he wrote, "Last Sunday we could hear the firing distinctly in the western part of the state ...We heard it till after sundown..."[25]

A more immediate consequence of the battle was 23,000 Union and Confederate casualties — the bloodiest harvest for any single day's fighting of the war. For weeks after the battle, the human carnage remained to be seen in field hospitals as army surgeons and civilian volunteers struggled to care for the wounded of both armies. Nearly 50 miles to the west at the Frederick Depot of the Baltimore and Ohio Railroad, thousands of wounded awaited the journey to Baltimore where makeshift hospitals were quickly established. Not since the War of 1812 when British expeditionary forces attacked the city had Baltimore felt the impact of war upon its population. Overnight the city had become a vast complex of medical facilities that spurred the use of Fort McHenry as a temporary prison and hospital. Medical reports for July 1862 recorded 1,780 sick and disabled soldiers under treatment in the city. Another 1,016 were within the grounds of Fort McHenry of which 814 were convalescent Union soldiers. The number of new arrivals would soon overwhelm the garrison and city resources.[26]

The influx of wounded prompted the federal government to lease Point Lookout, a popular resort in Southern Maryland at the confluence of the Potomac River and the Chesapeake, for a Union hospital. Within a year the site would be converted to one of the North's largest prison facilities. On October 18, *The Sun* chronicled the arrival of one of many trains carrying Confederate prisoners:

> "*Arrival of Confederate Prisoners.*— Last evening, shortly after 8 o'clock, two trains of burthen cars, in all about sixty in number, reached the Camden Station of the B&O Railroad, having on board from 12 to 14 hundred Rebel prisoners captured in the recent engagements in Western Maryland...."[27]

By the end of October, an estimated 2,000 Confederate prisoners had been sent to Baltimore, the majority being transferred by steamers to Fort Monroe or to Aiken's Landing on the James River to be exchanged. On December 8, all Confederate prisoners had been transferred south. At the fort's post hospital, Medical Director Dr. Simpson, indicated there were no more than 50 patients under treatment.[28]

Such was the response to the wounded and prisoners, that the fort's commander, General Morris issued the following order: "Hereafter no person or carriage whatsoever will be permitted within the gates of Fort McHenry with clothing or provisions to the Rebel prisoners. Supplies of this kind will be deposited with the guard at the exterior gate for that office, where they will be duly distributed to those requiring this aid."[29]

McClellan's lost opportunities on the Peninsula campaign near Richmond, and the tactical standoff at Antietam, prompted Lincoln to visit him in the field. On October 1, Lincoln boarded a special train provided by Robert W. Garrett, President of the Baltimore and Ohio Railroad. Garrett accompanied the President. Passing through Relay Station the Presidential party reached Harpers Ferry, from whence they were conveyed to the camp of the Army of the Potomac.

For four days, McClellan and the President toured the battlefield and visited the wounded of both armies. Lincoln ordered McClellan to pursue Lee, but he did not move until October 26, and then at such a slow pace

Robert W. Garrett: President of the Baltimore and Ohio Railroad during the Civil War.

as to cause the enemy no harm. Exasperated, Lincoln replaced McClellan on November 5, with the hero of "Burnside Bridge," Major General Ambrose Burnside. The little Napoleon had fought his last battle.

By November 18, Burnside had moved the federal army to Falmouth, Virginia, in pursuit of Lee. Crossing the river to storm the heights of Fredericksburg on December 13, Burnside's army of 100,000 men were repulsed with heavy losses. Victory continued to elude the federal army in Virginia at the end of 1862.

In Baltimore, on December 23, Major General Robert C. Schenck replaced General Wool as commander of the Middle Department. *The Baltimore American* proclaimed on Christmas Day "....almost any change ...would have been hailed with acclamations." Schenck was not from the Regular Army and it was hoped that he would be more lenient toward the city's population. Governor Bradford and a group of Union men held a banquet for the new department commander on January 23, in an attempt to begin anew.

It was soon discovered that Schenck brought with him not only the heavy hand of a military dictator, but the personal objectives of a political general seeking public office. Prior to the war the native Ohioan had served four terms in Congress, then was Minister to Brazil from 1851-53. After the war, his political savvy would land him the position of U.S. Minister to the Court of St. James in London. In his present position as commander of the department, he would use his provost marshal, Major William S. Fish to neutralize his opposition and that of his party's with politically motivated arrests.[30]

1863

*I*n March the Congress of the United States granted President Lincoln the power to suspend the writ of habeas corpus as a special wartime measure. This was almost two years after Lincoln had assumed such power with the arrest of John Merryman.[31]

On March 7, Schenck issued an order prohibiting the sale of secession music and required the publishers to send their remaining inventories to his headquarters. Four days later the sale of Rebel soldiers or statesmen photographs was also forbidden. His actions were endorsed by the City Union Convention. In June, Schenck closed the Maryland Club, declaring that it was a "...resort for those disaffected toward the government, hostile to its legally constituted authorities, and who give countenance, encouragement, and aid to the unnatural and causeless rebellion..." The Alston Association Club and the Germania Club soon met the same fate.[32]

Following the Southern victories at Fredericksburg and Chancellorsville, Virginia, General Robert E. Lee decided on an offensive in the North, confident of obtaining a decisive victory. On June 14, the Army of Northern Virginia moved northward from Fredericksburg, beginning a month long campaign that would culminate at the crossroads of Gettysburg. Dividing the Rebel army into three corps, Lee moved through the Shenandoah Valley, and by the 24th crossed the Potomac River at Shepardstown, West Virginia. The Army of the Potomac under Hooker followed in close pursuit from Fairfax, Virginia. On June 23, Union forces skirmished with Lee's First and Second corps in Western Maryland, prompting Lincoln to call for 100,000 volunteers to repel the Southern invasion.

One regiment that responded to this emergency call up was the Seventh New York National Guard under the command of Colonel Marshall Lefferts. The New Yorkers arrived at President Street Station on the morning of May 18, packed in cattle cars provided by the Philadelphia, Wilmington, and Baltimore Railroad. It was assigned to the Second Separate Brigade under General Morris.

The next day the regiment was dispersed throughout the city performing duties for the provost marshal's office. Twenty men from Company K, under the command of Lieutenant Joseph Lentilhon guarded provisions en route to Fort McHenry. Three full companies under Captain Charles Easton of Company I escorted 1,200 prisoners from the Baltimore and Ohio Depot to a steamer waiting at dockside to convey them to Fort Delaware.

On the 20th the regiment was assigned to Fort Federal Hill where it had seen service the previous summer. No sooner had the guardsmen marched into the Fort than Colonel Lefferts received orders to send his teamsters with all available spades and pickaxes to Lieutenant Meigs of the Engineers at the intersection of Lansdale Street and Pennsylvania Avenue. Later the same day Lefferts received a directive from General Morris concerning the defense of the city during the pending crisis.

Head-quarters Second Separate Brigade, Eighth Army Corps, Defense of Baltimore, Fort McHenry, June 20, 1863.

Colonel Marshall Lefferts, Commanding Fort Federal Hill. Colonel, — I am instructed by the general commanding to send you (30) thirty rockets, to be used as signals, if occasion should require. Should an approach of the enemy, or any other event, render it important, in your opinion, to summon the garrisons at Forts McHenry and Marshall to arms, three rockets will be sent up by you at intervals of two minutes. The sentinels at your post will be instructed accordingly. The same order is given at this post and at Fort Marshall, and obeyed at your post.

By command of Brigadier-General Morris, U.S.A.,

E.W. Andrews,

Captain and Acting Assistant Adjutant-General.

At 11 o'clock on the night of June 27, Colonel William H. Chesebrough of General Schenck's staff arrived at Fort Federal Hill with instructions for a strong force of infantry to proceed at once to the Maryland Club and arrest anyone found there. It was felt that if Lee's army approached Baltimore, the pro-Southern members of this organization would in some way aid in his capturing the city.

Twenty minutes later a detachment from companies B and E were double-quicking it toward Mount Vernon Square, bent on capturing those engaged in ". . . treason, stratagem, and spoils." There, in the shadows of the Washington Monument, they found the building locked and no one on the premises. The New Yorkers believed their attempted arrest had been foiled by a tip off to the club members. It is also possible that the members were never there in the first place, and their only crime was to be asleep in the beds dreaming of a Confederate victory.[33]

Near midnight on June 29, Baltimore was thrown into excitement due to reports that Confederate cavalry were on the outskirts of the city. The day before, three cavalry brigades were detached from the main Rebel army and crossed the Potomac at Edward's Ferry, entering Rockville at 11 a.m. Capturing 125 Union supply wagons, Stuart proceeded northward through Cooksville cutting telegraph lines and burning rail bridges. Continuing north in search of Lee, he occupied Westminster on the 29th and 30th engaging and capturing a small detachment of the 150th New York Infantry. Continuing in to Pennsylvania, he set fire to the barracks at Carlisle and then turned west on July 2 to rejoin Lee.

The presence of the enemy cavalry in Maryland prompted rumors that a large Rebel force was descending on the city. An officer of the Seventh New York stationed on Federal Hill observed the effect upon the populace of Baltimore:

"The alarm commenced with the violent ringing of the city bells, which soon followed by three rockets, the signal of danger, from Forts McHenry, Marshall and Federal Hill. At the first note of alarm the loyal citizens of Baltimore thronged the streets and hastened with their arms to the barricades and the earth works,

"Citizens of Baltimore barricading the streets, Monday evening, June 29th, 1863" is the title of this engraving from *Leslie's Illustrated Newspaper.*

which had been erected for the defense of the city. Non-combatants could not resist this storm of excitement, but ventured forth to canvas the news or witness the arrival of the enemy, while women and children from windows and behind shutters peered timidly upon the thousands that rushed madly through the streets .... An hour of patient waiting convinced the officers that the danger of an attack was not imminent ...The cause of this great excitement was said to be the advance guard of a body of hostile [Rebel] cavalry to within a few miles of Baltimore..."[34]

In preparation, Commodore Thomas Dormin, commanding the Baltimore Naval District placed several U.S. Gunboats, the *Eutaw, Philadelphia, Marayanza* and *Seymour,* to bear their guns upon the city's main avenues. Members of the black population were impressed to build barricades and all loyal Union men were organized and armed to meet the rebels.[35]

In Gettysburg, on July 3, both armies clashed following an immense artillery cannonade which, like Antietam nine months before, was heard in Baltimore as "distant thunder." Robert E. Lee's invasion had been repulsed as remnants of Longstreet's ill-fated assault upon the Union lines at Cemetery Ridge returned to their lines.

"The good news from Gettysburg," a Union officer wrote, "made all hearts rejoice; not so much that Baltimore was safe, as that the country was safe, as that the whelming tide of invasion [was] turned." No sooner had Baltimoreans displayed Independence Day banners then the tragic results of the battle arrived. Thousands of wounded soldiers and prisoners overwhelmed the city's rail depots. The scene must have been one of contrast amidst patriotic displays as relief measures were undertaken to receive the wounded. On July 6, *The Sun* in its daily recording of prisoner of war arrivals stated:

> "*Arrival of Confederate Prisoners.*— There were yesterday heavy arrivals of Confederate prisoners captured in the late battles. In the forenoon, a body of seven hundred reached the city over the Western Maryland Railroad, and at eight o'clock last night another train containing upwards of 2400 reached the Bolton depot. Those who arrived in the afternoon and those who arrived last night were marched to Fort McHenry to await transportation for exchange. There are said to still be 700 Confederate prisoners at Westminster awaiting transportation to this city, and they will reach here to-day. Thus far about 4000 have arrived."[36]

In the weeks afterward, the numbers established the enormity of the conflict by the arrival of more prisoners of war that included Major General Isaac Ridgeway Trimble, C.S.A., and Brigadier General James Lawson Kemper, C.S.A., both were seriously wounded on July 3, and later confined at Fort McHenry.

The Wests Buildings on Pratt Street became one of the first and largest buildings to be utilized as a hospital following the Battle of Antietam in 1862. Now a year later, Gettysburg veteran, Private Henry Shepard C.S.A., wounded at Culps Hill, recorded his impressions of the former cotton warehouse as "...dark, gloomy, without adequate ventilation, devoid of sanitary or hygienic appliances or conveyances, and pervaded at all times by the pestilential exhalations which arose from the neighboring docks..."[37]

Union soldiers escorted Rebel prisoners along a three mile march to Fort McHenry, while ambulances, carriages and wagons carried the wounded in a continuous procession from morning to night. At Fort McHenry, officials quickly converted three, two-storied brick stables into temporary prisons. Hundreds of prisoners were guarded upon the open parade grounds surrounding the fort while awaiting transfer. During the first two weeks of July the number of prisoners sent to Fort McHenry soared to 6,795. From the 18th to the 30th an additional 162 arrived, bringing the total to 6,957. By August only 54 remained.[38]

The unexpected arrivals prompted the establishment of a permanent federal prison at Point Lookout in St. Mary's County where a hospital had been established in 1862. Here the majority of all Gettysburg prisoners were sent. Others went to Fort Delaware. Point Lookout would rival the Confederate prison at Andersonville, Georgia, in numbers it held and buried by the spring of 1865 — 20,000 Confederates were imprisoned at the Point, of which nearly 4,000 died.[39]

Of all the Confederates sent to Baltimore, the remains of Brigadier General Lewis Addison Armistead, Pickett's Division, is the most noted. Armistead was among the hundred or so Confederates who survived the assault and breached the Union lines on Cemetery Ridge before the overwhelming Union musketry ended their brief moment of glory at Gettysburg, the high water mark of the Confederacy.

Armistead was wounded in the arm and leg, but neither were considered serious by the Union surgeon who attended him. The general also suffered from overexertion and mental anxiety. He died two days later in a field hospital on the Spangler Farm where he was buried. A month later his remains were removed by friends and taken to Baltimore. He was buried in St. Paul's Cemetery next to his famous uncle, Lieutenant Colonel George Armistead, the commander of Fort McHenry during the War of 1812. The hero of Gettysburg now laid with the hero of Fort McHenry.[40]

On June 30, when it was learned that Lee's army was again across the Potomac River, General Schenck declared martial law throughout the state of Maryland. Both Loyalists and Rebels had to contend with

(Craig Horn)

Brig. Gen. Lewis A. Armistead: Killed at Gettysburg, he was buried next to his uncle who had commanded Fort McHenry during the War of 1812.

restricted travel and business hours. On July 2, things got worse when it became unlawful for a private citizen to have a firearm in his home unless he was enrolled in a militia company. Schenck did not release these harsh measures until late November in order to better control the outcome of the state elections.[41]

On September 11, Schenck ordered the *Baltimore Republican* to cease operations and arrested the editor and owner, Mr. Beale H. Richardson, and his associate editors, Francis A. Richardson and Stephen J. Joyce. All three men were taken into custody by the provost marshal and sent south via Harpers Ferry. They were warned that if they returned they would be arrested as spies. Their crime was the publication of a poem by Mrs. Ellen Key Blunt entitled "The Southern Cross." Before the end of the month the *Baltimore Daily Gazette* was also ordered to stop the presses and its owners, Edward F. Carter and William H. Neilson were arrested. On the 29th, two publishers of the *Catholic Mirror*, Mr. Michael J. Kelly and John B. Piet, were arrested by government detectives and charged with selling the pamphlet *"Fourteen Months in the American Bastille,"* by Frank Key Howard. Arrests also extended to the clergy. Reverend Thomas H. Pritchard of the Franklin Square Baptist Church was arrested on the charge of "attempting to go south."

On October 9, Provost Marshal Fish ordered the seizures of all pictures, stationery and envelopes which represented the different fortifications in and about the city of Baltimore. Bookstore owners were warned not to offer any such items for sale.[42]

State elections to elect a new state comptroller and members of the General Assembly were held on November 4, 1863. General Schenck controlled the outcome as best he could by issuing General Order No. 53 which placed soldiers at the polling places and authorized the arrest of any

Publ. by Chas Magnus N.Y.

Belger Barracks, Baltimore, Md. (1)

PARODY ON
The Cottage by the Sea.

By EUGENE T. JOHNSTON.

"Childhood's days have passed before me,"
   Dear Tom, "Just twenty years ago ;"
"Tis Columbia's greatest glory "
   "Paddy's Museum" and "Baby-Show,"
"When this cruel war is over,"
   "Sally is the gal for me ;"
"Thou hast learned to love another,"
   "In the cottage by the sea,"
   "Let me kiss him for his mother,"
   "In the cottage by the sea,"

"We are coming, Sister Mary,"
   In "The Irish jaunting-car."
"Hold your horses," "Paddy Carey,"
   "There is whiskey in the jar."
"Here I am, as you diskiver"—
   "Maiden, wilt thou dwell with me,"
'Near the banks of that lone river,"
   "In the cottage by the sea?"
   "Our starry flag shall wave forever,"
   "In the cottage by the sea."

"Since I've been in the army,"
   "In the days of old lang syne,"
Near "The pleasant groves of Blarney"
   "I'd offer thee this hand of mine."
"The old gray mare" sleeps "In the valley"—
   She was "The belle of Avenue B,"
"No one to love" but "Old Aunt Sally,"
   "In the cottage by the sea,"
   To "Limerick Races" "Freemen rally,"
   "In the cottage by the sea."

"Alice Gray," "Last Rose of Summer,"
   "We'll meet again" at "Donnybrook Fair,"
"Come into my cabin, old bummer,"
   For you're "The boy with the auburn hair."
You're "Played out" "Sweet highland Mary,"
   Since "Dorans Ass" went "On a spree;"
With "The men of Tipperary,"
   "In the cottage by the sea."
   And sweet "William of the Ferry,"
   "In the cottage by the sea."

   "We have lived and loved together"
      On "the Yankee man-of war;"
   "With a jockey hat and feather,"
      "Thou art so near, and yet so far,"
   "One good turn deserves another"—
      Then O "Woodmann, spare that tree !"
   "What is home without a mother,"
      "In the cottage by the sea ?"
      "Bryan O'Lynn," "Scorn not thy brother,"
      "In the cottage by the sea."

(D.C.T.)

During the war a wide range of illustrations depicting the forts and camps around Baltimore were made to sell to the soldiers stationed in the city. Many contained such details as number and location of cannon, regimental assignments and headquarters location. Better than aerial photographs for Rebel spies, Provost Marshal Fish ordered them confiscated in 1863.

person known or thought to be disloyal. This, combined with the extravagant use of martial law since July, ensured a victory for the Union Party.[43]

Four months after the Battle of Gettysburg, on November 16, eight companies of the Fifth New York Artillery left their camp at Fort Marshall to accompany President Lincoln as he passed through Baltimore en route to Gettysburg, where he was to address the crowd with "a few appropriate remarks" at the consecration ceremonies of the new Soldiers' National Cemetery. A week later on November 26 the nation held it's first national observance of a day of Thanksgiving.

On November 30, ex-Governor Thomas G. Pratt and his secretary, Colonel Joseph Nicholson, were sent south via Fortress Monroe for refusing to take the oath of allegiance. Also in November the 80-year-old mother of Confederate General John H. Winder was arrested when she received a letter from her granddaughter in North Carolina. The letter was intercepted by a federal agent and taken to Mrs. Gertrude Winder. When she accepted the letter she was arrested for communicating with the enemy and taken to the provost marshal's office in a driving rainstorm. After her son explained the circumstances of the case she was granted parole and returned home only to have her residence raided again just after Christmas.[44]

General Schenck left Baltimore City in November to take a seat in Congress from the state of Ohio. He was temporarily replaced by General Henry H. Lockwood. A native of Delaware, Lockwood had commanded a brigade in the Middle Department which operated in the Eastern Shore counties of Maryland and Virginia.

The wife of the President, Mary Todd Lincoln, paid a visit to Baltimore in company with her two sisters and mother, Mrs. R. S. Todd. They arrived aboard the steamer Louisiana on December 11 while that Old Bay Line vessel was under government contract.[45]

1864

In January the Baltimore Academy of Music and the Baltimore, Hall's Springs, and Harford Passenger Railway were granted charters by the General Assembly. On the 24th of the month, the provost marshal of Baltimore, Colonel William S. Fish, was arrested by order of the Secretary of War on charges of fraud and corruption. Fish and his accomplices made a business of arresting innocent people and then interceding on their behalf for a price. An example of this activity can be found in the case of Dr. Aaron Friedenwald. Dr. Friedenwald was the only Unionist member of a leading Jewish family. When the war broke out he was in Europe and did not return until 1862. Almost a year later he was arrested for running the blockade. Word soon reached the family that for the sum of $50,00 the doctor could gain his release. Fish was court-martialed and sent to prison in Albany, New York.[46]

On March 12, Major General Lew Wallace assumed command of the Middle Department. Wallace's first tour of duty in Maryland came in June 1861, when as a colonel he occupied Cumberland with the Eleventh Regiment of Indiana Zouaves. A division commander under Grant at Fort Donelson, he was promoted to major general, but fell out of favor with Grant after the battle of Shiloh. More flexible than the old Regular, Wool, and less occupied with politics than

(D.C.T.)

Maj. Gen. Lew Wallace: Commanded the Middle Department in 1864.

the scheming Schenck, he would prove to be an able and fair administrator as well as a good field general. After the war ended Wallace served on the commission that tried the Lincoln conspirators and was later president of the board that court-martialed and hanged Henry Wirz for war crimes at Andersonville. His greatest fame would come in 1880 when he authored the biblical novel *Ben Hur*.[47]

When Wallace took command General Schenck wrote him a letter in which he paid Baltimore the highest possible compliment and at the same time, albeit through his own frustration, revealed the very essence of life in Maryland during the Civil War.

"Your trouble will have origin in Baltimore. Baltimore viewed socially is peculiar. There is more culture to the square block than in Boston; actual culture. The question of war divided the old families, but I was never able to discover the dividing line. Did I put a heavy hand on one of the Secessionists, a delegation of influential Unionists at once hurried to the President and begged the culprit off.... There is another thing you should know, without being left to find it out experimentally, Baltimore is headquarters for a traffic in supply for Rebel armies the extent of which is simply incredible. It is an industry the men have nothing to do with. They know better, and leave it entirely to the women, who are cunning beyond belief, and bold on account of their sex."

General Wallace made his headquarters in the home of Reverdy Johnson opposite the Battle Monument. The day-to-day management of the city was left to Provost Marshal General John Woolley. Colonel Woolley appointed Captain H. B. Smith of the Fifth New York Heavy Artillery as chief of his Secret Service department. Smith directed the activities of 40 male and female spies, and became proficient in the game of counter-espionage. The provost marshal's department was located at the southwest corner of Camden and Eutaw Streets. It consisted of a three-story brick building adjacent to a former slave pen, known as "Donovans." The slave pen was converted to a military prison. Colonel Woolley had his office on the second floor of the brick building. Secret Service operations were run out of an office on the third floor. A three

Lt. Col. John Woolley: Provost Marshal of Baltimore 1864-1865.

story extension on the back was utilized as a barracks for troops assigned to provost marshal duty.

As a result of years of predatory arrests by previous department commanders, the jails in Baltimore, especially the old penitentiary, were bulging with prisoners. One of General Wallace's first orders was to review each case and immediately release any person who was held without sufficient evidence to stand trail.[48]

On April 6, Marylanders voted to rewrite the state's constitution. A major consideration would be the prohibition of slavery. Despite the absence of a large number of pro-Southern men from the state, the vote was less than overwhelming with 31,593 for and 19,524 against. State Comptroller Henry H. Goldsborough was elected president of

Capt. H. B. Smith: Chief detective in the Middle Department 1864-1865. After the war he wrote an account of his activities entitled *Between the Lines*.

the Constitutional Convention that convened in Annapolis on April 27.[49]

The high water mark of Union patriotism in Baltimore, if not in fact the entire state, may have been reached in the spring of 1864 when the Maryland State Fair for U.S. Soldier Relief was held between April 18 and May 2. Commonly referred to as the Baltimore Sanitary Fair, it was the result of a collaboration between two great benevolent organizations in the city; the United States Sanitary Commission and the United

States Christian Commission. The idea of a fair in Baltimore was first put forth by two members of the Ladies Union Relief Association, Mrs. Ann Bowen and Mrs. Fanny Turnbull. Mrs. Turnbull was also a member of the Sanitary Commission. They were soon joined in their efforts by Mrs. Harriet Hyatt, a member of the Christian Commission. Both organizations had active Baltimore Chapters that had sent aid to soldiers in Pennsylvania, Maryland, and Virginia as well as the hospitals and prisoners within the city. Other fairs had been held in northern cities like Chicago, but for the ladies of Baltimore the task was more daunting. Throughout the war Baltimore remained a divided city. Many of the wealthy upper class that would have been unified in a city like Boston were either serving in the Confederate army or living in exile. Those Southern sympathizers still residing in the city would be ambivalent toward its success. Finally, the government's reactions to military emergencies had often curtailed the day-to-day business activities of the merchants causing many financial hardships.

With great industry the loyal ladies met throughout the winter of 1862 to plan and solicit aid for the project. Each county in the state was invited to form a committee and participate in the event. A nationwide appeal went out for money, food, household goods, and war relics to be sold at the fair. In order to encourage statewide attendance, railroad and steamship companies agreed to special discounted rates for fair goers and the Adams Express Company (the U.P.S. of the 1860's) delivered donated items to the fair at no charge.[50]

Mrs. Elmira Lincoln Phelps, the corresponding secretary of the fair committee, requested many notable persons of the time to submit short stories, articles and poems concerning the history of the country and the war. These she edited into a book of over 400 pages entitled *Our Country* which was sold to benefit the project. The book was dedicated

"To the Mothers, Wives, and Sisters of the Loyal States, whose Sons, Husbands, and Brothers are periling their

(D.C.T.)

Mrs. Almira L. Phelps: Edited the book *Our Country* to raise money during the Sanitary Fair in 1864.

lives in the cause of the Country, in the Armies and Navies of the United States, with the prayer that the objects of their affection may, in God's good time, be restored to them, crowned with triumph and rewarded with the blessings of their grateful fellow-citizens, this volume is affectionately dedicated by the women of Maryland, through their State Fair Organization."[51]

In order to gain the broadest possible base of support, the fair was co-chaired by Mr. William J. Albert, a strong leader in the German community and member of the Unconditional Union Party in the state, and Mrs. Elizabeth Bradford, wife of the Governor. As a final touch President Lincoln was invited to attend the opening ceremonies and spend the evening at the home of Mr. Albert. The fair opened on April 18, 1864. The coincidence of the date cannot be overlooked for on this same date

(D.C.T.)

President Abraham Lincoln: His only overnight stay in the city came in 1864 when he delivered a speech on the opening night of the Sanitary Fair.

three years earlier Pennsylvania soldiers moving through the city were stoned by a mob and Nickoles Biddle, a free black man, became the first casualty of the war. At 2:00 p.m. a parade of 3,000 soldiers left Monument Square and marched through the city to the music of the Eighth New York and Second U.S. Artillery bands. Nearly 30,000 persons lined the streets to cheer them on and wave Old Glory. A second parade followed containing the same number of black volunteers from Maryland's newly raised regiments of United States Colored Troops.[52]

At 6:00 p.m., the President's train arrived at Camden Station. He was taken by carriage to the Maryland Institute on East Baltimore Street, the site of the fair. Governor Bradford addressed the audience first, then Mrs. Bradford escorted the President to the platform for a short speech before touring the hall. The first portion of his speech concerned the changes in the city.

> "Ladies and Gentlemen — Calling to mind that we are here in Baltimore, we cannot fail to note that the world moves. Looking upon these many people, assembled here, to serve, as they best may, the soldiers of the Union, it occurs at once that three years ago, the same soldiers could not so much as pass through Baltimore. The change from then till now, is both great and gratifying. Blessings on the brave men who have wrought the change, and the fair women who strive to reward them for it. But Baltimore suggests more than could happen within Baltimore. The change within Baltimore is part only of a far wider change. When the war began, three years ago, neither party, nor any man, expected it would last till now. Each looked for the end, in some way, long ere to-day. Neither did any anticipate that domestic slavery would be much affected by the war. But here we are; the war has not ended, and slavery has been much affected — how much needs not now be recounted. So true is it that man proposes, and God disposes."[53]

After visiting many of the booths and talking to a great number of people he left the hall at 11:00 p.m. and went to the home of Mr. Albert where he spent the night. The next day he returned to Washington. On the 20th Mrs. Lincoln attended the fair accompanied by President Robert Garrett of the Baltimore and Ohio Railroad. Throughout the course of the event a number of dignitaries, both domestic and foreign, took the train from Washington to attend the fair. Soldiers from nearby hospitals also attended as semi-guests of honor. The fair closed on May 2 and again Governor Bradford addressed the attendees. When it was over the Loyal Women of Maryland had raised $80,000 for the soldiers and sailors of the United States. More importantly this had shown the nation that a large portion of the state's population supported the Union. No longer could the Northern press paint the city of Baltimore in a single shade of Confederate gray. They had also given the President an opportunity to enter the city with dignity and to some extent atone for his nocturnal transit in February of 1861.[54]

The Presidential election of 1864 prompted the Republicans to chose Baltimore City as the site for their national convention, as the Democrats had used Baltimore earlier in the ante-bellum years. With the war far from over in the spring of 1864, it was important to keep travel time away from the seat of government to a minimum for the President and members of Congress. The Republican National Convention convened at the Front Street Theatre on June 7 and lasted for only one day. Abraham Lincoln was nominated for President and Andrew Johnson of Tennessee for Vice-President. Henry W. Hoffman, chairman of the Maryland delegation, had the honor of seconding Lincoln's nomination.[55]

By the summer of 1864 the defenses of both Washington and Baltimore were stripped of men as all but a few units in each were sent to replace the huge losses General Ulysses Grant was sustaining in Virginia as his army fought its way through the Wilderness to erect siege lines at Petersburg. Immobilized and outnumbered, Lee sent Lieutenant General Jubal A. Early and the much diminished Second Corps to Lynchburg at the head of the Shenandoah Valley. His orders were to drive off the Union army under General David Hunter, move down the length of the valley and, if possible, cross the Potomac River and threaten the cities of Baltimore or Washington as the opportunity presented itself.

*T*he third and final Confederate invasion of Maryland began on the 4th of July when Early led the survivors of Jackson's once feared valley army into Western Maryland. His total force numbered no more than 10,000 to 15,000 men. One of his cavalry brigades was commanded by newly promoted General Bradley T. Johnson who in April 1861 had marched his mounted militia from Frederick City to answer the call of Marshall Kane.

The Confederates were successful in both speed and deception. Grant was not convinced that Early had left the Petersburg lines until he was nearly in position to attack Harpers Ferry. His cavalry operated in a wide arch in front of the main force causing Department Commander

Lew Wallace to believe Early's force numbered 20,000 to 30,000 men. Wallace began to receive information about Early's advance during the first week of June. John Garrett's telegraphers and train crews sent a steady stream of reports to the B&O president who in turn passed the information on to General Wallace. Lincoln was also getting nervous and authorized a number of states, including Maryland, to raise emergency regiments to serve for a term of 100 days.[56]

The Eleventh Maryland Infantry was recruited in mid-June in Baltimore City under the command of Colonel William T. Landstreet. The city fathers encouraged this activity with a $50 enlistment bonus. There is reason to believe that the nucleus of this regiment was formed by Baltimore City Guard Battalion, a pro-Union militia organization that maintained its identity throughout the war. This regiment of citizen-soldiers was mustered into the army at Camp Bradford on June 16. From there they were sent to Camp Carroll for a brief period of training before being sent to Relay where they were issued 40 rounds of ammunition and boarded a special train for Monocacy Junction on the night of July 5.[57]

The western boundary of the Middle Department in 1864 was the Monocacy River. Frederick City was west of the river. General Wallace could have easily remained in the defenses of Baltimore and declared that the Rebels were outside his department. To his credit he realized that to give up 50 miles of Maryland countryside and B&O trackage to the enemy would not only invite its destruction, but leave the door wide open for an attack on the nation's capital. Without informing General Halleck in Washington, Wallace began to shift his meager forces to Monocacy Junction. These included the Eleventh Maryland Infantry, six guns of Alexander's Battery, and a few companies of Ohio volunteers. At the Junction he joined forces with Brigadier General Erastus B. Tyler in an attempt to save the city of Frederick from the Rebels. Their multi-state force of volunteers numbered only about 2,500 men.[58]

By now General Grant had dispatched the Sixth Army Corps to reinforce both Baltimore and Washington. The division of Brigadier General James B. Ricketts sailed up the Chesapeake Bay and landed at Locust Point, adjacent to Fort McHenry, on July 7 and 8. Two brigades arrived at Monocacy Junction on the 8th giving Wallace 6,000 men and seven guns to face Early's force still believed to number in the tens of thousands. Wallace was convinced Early was headed for Washington. He extended his force out along the banks of the Monocacy River and placed the veterans of the Sixth Corps on his left flank where the fighting was sure to be the heaviest. Early attacked on the morning of July 9.

Pvt. William Forsyth: Co. B, Third Battalion Baltimore City Guards.

At the end of the day-long battle, Wallace's little army was pushed aside and Early was on the road to Washington where he would be the proverbial day late, but not a dollar short thanks to his ransoming of Frederick City for $200,000.[59]

When Early reached the outskirts of Washington, he found the balance of the Sixth Corps filing into the city's fortifications. After a brief siege designed to allow Bradley Johnson's cavalry time to rejoin the main force, Early led his army back into Virginia. When the magnitude of Wallace's gamble became known, he was vindicated for his actions and allowed to keep his position as department commander.

While Wallace's miniature army fought to save Washington, the city of Baltimore was in a state of near panic. When word reached the city of Wallace's defeat, citizens took to the streets to discuss matters and await the latest wire dispatches. A committee of city officials sent a telegram to Lincoln begging for troops to refill the empty defenses of Baltimore. The sale of alcohol was restricted and orders were issued to impress horses for the use of the army. A quota was even levied on the City Passenger Railroad Company. The next morning residents of Baltimore awoke to ringing church bells and a joint proclamation by Governor Bradford and Mayor Chapman declaring the city in eminent danger. General Lockwood, in a role similar to General Isaac Trimbles' in 1861, was put in charge of a civilian defense force called out to man existing fortifications and erect new ones wherever needed. Loyal men, both black and white, formed their respective companies and were issued arms after which they were sent to various parts of the line. The City Council appropriated $100,000 for the construction of additional fortifications. The Board of Police Commissioners reacted to the crisis by adding 400 additional policemen to the force. There was no time to issue uniforms, only badges and ribbons to denote their special status. Concerned about a Confederate advance from the west, a large number of B&O locomotives were transferred from the main branch and Mount Clare depot to the tracks on Pratt Street.[60]

There was no shortage of generals to give orders in Wallace's absence. Halleck assigned General Morris to the overall defense of the city on July 9. Morris put General Lockwood in charge of the civilian volunteers. Two days later Halleck gave Major General Edward O.C. Ord command of the Eighth Army Corps and all the troops in the Middle Department. Ord, a native of Cumberland, Maryland, was a Regular Army officer and West Point graduate. He ordered all bars and restaurants in the city closed. No ship was allowed to clear the harbor without obtaining a permit first. Civilian travel in and out of the city was severely restricted causing a sharp rise in market prices.

72

On July 12, Governor Bradford ordered John S. Berry, the state adjutant general, to call out the Maryland Militia. The mobilization took two days. By then the crisis had passed. General Wallace had returned to Baltimore and General Early was making preparations to return to Virginia. It is ironic that with each passing day as the Rebel army moved further away from Baltimore, the city took greater steps to defend itself. This may have been in part caused by a secondary Confederate operation known as the Johnson-Gilmor Raid.[61]

(D.C.T.)

Maj. Gen. E.O.C. Ord: Commanded the Eighth Army Corps and all troops in the Middle Department immediately after the Battle of Monocacy.

One portion of Early's army not committed to the battle on July 9, was the cavalry brigade of Bradley T. Johnson. Johnson had recently been promoted to brigadier general and given the command of Brigadier General William E. Jones' brigade when that officer was killed at the battle of Piedmont, Virginia, on June 5. Added to the brigade were the First and Second Maryland Cavalry battalions under the command of Major Harry Gilmor and the Baltimore Light Artillery. Gilmor was a resident of Baltimore County and would be the point man for the operations in that area.

Johnson's mission was one of the truly great "might have beens" of the war. The plan called for a naval expedition to slip out of the port at Wilmington, North Carolina, and sail up the coast to Point Lookout, Maryland, where over 10,000 Confederate prisoners of war were held. In the hold of the two blockade runners were two field pieces and thousands of muskets with which to arm the prisoners when they were released. Also aboard the ships were 800 Confederate sailors and marines under the command of General George Washington Custis Lee. Lee was to attack the prison camp from the bay side while Johnson hit them from inland. To get there his brigade was first to ride north of Baltimore and cut the Northern Central Railroad, then reverse its march and travel through central Maryland to the southern tip of St. Mary's County at

Point Lookout. "D- Day" was set for July 12. This meant an incredible march of nearly 200 miles in only ninety-six hours with no extra time for fighting or sleeping.

At dawn on July 9, Johnson's command was at Wormans Mill about two miles north of Frederick on the Old Liberty Road. As soon as it became evident that Early would win the Battle of Monocacy, Johnson struck off in the direction of New Windsor, in Carroll County. There they set fire to the bridge and station belonging to the Western Maryland Railroad. Gilmor, with twenty men, was sent ahead to Westminster to cut the telegraph wires. The next day Johnson's men reached Cockeysville. After setting fire to the bridges on the Northern Central Railroad, Gilmor was ordered to continue on with about 135 men from the two Maryland Battalions. His mission was to burn the drawbridge that carried the Philadelphia, Wilmington and Baltimore Railroad over the Gunpowder River and in any other way possible disrupt communications between Baltimore and the North. Johnson then took the main Confederate force through the Greenspring Valley and camped near Owings Mills. Before heading south toward Point Lookout on July 11, he sent Lieutenant Henry Blackstone and twelve men from the First Maryland Cavalry to burn the home of Governor Bradford on North Charles Street. This action was in retaliation for the destruction of Governor John Letcher's home in Lexington, Virginia, by General Hunter.[62]

Gilmor played his part to the fullest. At Magnolia Station he captured two trains and a number of Union officers including Major General William B. Franklin. The first train was burned. The second was set ablaze and backed onto the bridge sending both smoking and hissing into the Bush River. Gilmor then paroled all the captured soldiers but four officers and General Franklin. These were loaded into a carriage with the idea of carrying them back to Virginia. Unfortunately for Gilmor, his guards fell asleep after almost 48 hours of continuous riding and all the prisoners escaped. Gilmor's last action was a skirmish with a cavalry patrol from the city near Towsontown. With so much Confederate activity north and west of the city, it is no wonder that the authorities in Baltimore could only think in terms of strengthening their defenses.[63]

By the end of August the city had returned to its normal wartime pace. On the last Sunday in July, the Right Reverend Martin J. Spalding, formerly of Louisville, Kentucky, was consecrated Archbishop of Baltimore at the Cathedral on Franklin Street. The colony of Maryland had been founded as a refuge for Catholics and the ever increasing number of Irish immigrants in the city made this a major non-military event in 1864.[64]

October saw a flurry of political activity leading up to the Presidential election the following month. On the 12th and 13th Marylanders went to the polls to vote on the new State Constitution which included the prohibition of slavery. Despite two years of federal occupation throughout the state, the referendum passed by only 375 votes. A day later, Chief Justice Roger Brooke Taney died at the age of eighty-eight. Taney had crossed legal swords with Lincoln at the gates of Fort McHenry over the arrest of John Merryman in 1861. He was buried in his home town of Frederick, Maryland.[65]

(D.C.T.)

Rev. Martin J. Spalding: Consecrated Archbishop of Baltimore in 1864. The large number of Irish immigrants living in the city made this a major event.

In mid-October, a plot was discovered by detectives in Provost Marshal Lt. Colonel John Woolley's command to alter the votes of New York soldiers in the Presidential election. On April 21, 1864, the State of New York passed legislation which allowed soldiers in the army to vote by proxy. The soldier would fill out his ballot and place it in a sealed envelope. He would then sign a Power of Attorney and that document would be placed in a second envelope with the sealed ballot and delivered to his regular polling place. Three men working at the New York State Agents Office on Fayette Street were arrested when it was learned that they were telling the soldiers that they were out of Lincoln ballots, but would soon receive a new supply. The soldier would sign the Power of Attorney and leave. The agents would then substitute a McClellan ballot and send it to New York. As soon as the facts were known to him, General Wallace attended a special cabinet meeting in Washington to appraise the President of the election frauds and warn Union commanders in other cities. Upon his return he personally wrote out the order to arrest Mr. M. J. Ferry, Edward Donohue, Jr., and any others implicated in the crime. Among the evidence found in Ferry's office was a bundle of counterfeit documents and a letter from John F. Semour, whose brother was governor of New York. On October 27, the affair was made known to the public and the newspapers referred to it as "The Great Soldiers Vote Fraud." The scandal caused a great embarrassment for the Northern Democrats on the eve of the election.[66]

The new state constitution took effect on the first day of November, 1864, and with it slavery ceased to exist in Maryland. On the 4th of the month, the Democrats held a mass meeting at the Maryland Institute Hall. Just as Albert Ritchie, a future governor of the state, called the meeting to order, federal soldiers broke into the hall and disrupted the meeting in a violent manner. Several of the speakers escaped by means of a rope down a rear hatchway onto Second Street.

General Wallace's reason for disrupting the meeting was that he had received word that their true intentions were to seize the armory on the corner of Baltimore and Frederick Streets and use the weapons to attack the soldiers garrisoning the city. As had happened before, a military excuse was given to legitimize an obvious politically motivated activity.[67]

The Presidential election took place on November 8. Lincoln carried the state of Maryland with his new running mate, Andrew Johnson, the former military governor of Tennessee appointed by Lincoln in 1862. On a local level Thomas Swann, a former mayor of Baltimore City, became the third wartime governor of Maryland. The day after the election, General Wallace issued General Order No. 112, which established a Freedman's Bureau to aid slaves recently freed by the new State Constitution on November 1. Major William F. Este was placed in charge of the Bureau and instructed to take possession of the now vacant Maryland Club House and utilize it as a reception center for sick and homeless ex-slaves. The building was renamed "Freedman's Rest."[68]

Considering the great impact the battle of July 9 had on the city of Baltimore, many citizens may have thought the name appropriate when the U.S.S. Monocacy was launched on December 14. Built by the firm of A.&W. Denmead & Son, she was an iron side-wheel steamer and carried six guns. The cost of construction was $275,000.[69]

Until the end of the war the provost marshal's office continued to evaluate the cases of spies, deserters, and refugees from the South. A true deserter would cross the lines wherever the opportunity presented itself. Spies and official couriers always began their missions from Richmond. Many of these passed through the Signal Corps station operated by Sergeant Harry Brogden on the Virginia side of the Potomac River. Brogden was once a prisoner at Fort McHenry. Captain Smith, Wallace's chief detective, tracked one man for a year before finally capturing him just before Christmas of 1864. Charles E. Langley posed as reporter for the New York *Tribune* in order to pass freely through the Union lines while on official business for the Confederacy. Smith called him "...one of the most expert and successful official spies..."[70]

(Smith)

Charles E. Langley: An expert Confederate spy, he posed as a reporter for the *New York Tribune*.

1865

The Confederacy would emerge from the winter of 1864 nearly defeated. At Petersburg, Grant waited for good weather before cracking Lee's defensive position and forcing the evacuation of Richmond on April 3, while Sherman stalked Joseph Johnson's army through the Carolinas. Philip Sheridan delivered the final blow in the Shenandoah Valley when he defeated the remnants of Early's army at Waynesboro on March 2, and then joined Grant for the final campaign against the Army of Northern Virginia.

In the closing days of the war an estimated 1,500 Confederate prisoners were sent to Baltimore. They came by rail in prison cars to the B&O station at Camden Street where they were unloaded and marched to Fort McHenry along what was then called the Fort Road.

Captain Smith's detective force scored a near miss on March 9, when they arrested Lewis Paine at 16 North Eutaw Street, the home of noted Rebel, Miss Maggie Branson. When interviewed the next day, Paine claimed to be a refugee from Fauquier County, Virginia and a cousin of Miss Branson. Smith later wrote "I felt in my bones he was a spy, but could not prove it." On the 12th, Paine took the oath of allegiance and Captain Smith granted him a parole with the stipulation that he go north of Philadelphia and remain there for the duration of the war. A month later, Paine was arrested for trying to kill Secretary of State William H. Seward in his home. When confronted at the home of Mary Surratt he produced the very same document he had been issued in Baltimore with the stipulation to go north.[71]

Before news of Grant's offensive operations reached Baltimore, a gale of biblical proportions blew through the city on the afternoon of March 23. Chimneys were toppled, trees uprooted, and fences knocked over. Several citizens were killed or injured as roofs were lifted off houses. The walls collapsed at the boiler shop of Murray and Weigrand on York Street burying the workmen in rubble and killing Philip Hughes.[72]

On April 1, the Battle of Five Forks was fought. The division of General George E. Pickett was destroyed by a combined attack of Sheridan's cavalry and Warren's Fifth Army Corps which included the Maryland Brigade. The next day Grant attacked all along the Petersburg line causing the Confederate government to abandon the city of Richmond that night. On April 3 word reached Baltimore that the Rebel capital had fallen and Lee's army was in retreat. Thousands took to the streets in jubilation. At 3 p.m., Mayor John L. Chapman ordered all the fire houses to unfurl their flags and ring their bells. The revelry lasted until midnight. On the 6th, the mayor and city council arranged a formal celebration. The city was draped in red, white and blue from one end to the other as bells rang and cannon boomed a thunderous salute. "It was indeed the brightest epoch that ever befell our city for those participating in the Union cause."[73]

By April 9, the Army of Northern Virginia could fight no more. Lee surrendered to Grant at Appomattox Courthouse. While the Unionists in the city rejoiced, those who had supported the Southern cause must have conceded to themselves that at least the war was over. In the next few days, dignitaries began to pass through the city.

On the 11th, Vice-Admiral David Farragut was greeted by the mayor and city council and General William Morris with a detachment of soldiers. The "Hero of Mobile Bay" was escorted to the Eutaw House where he briefly addressed the crowd. The next day he paid a visit to Fort McHenry and received a thirteen gun salute, commenting as he toured the garrison, "That Fort McHenry was not an easy place to take."

On the evening of the 14th, General and Mrs. Ulysses Grant passed through the city by train. Captain Smith of the provost marshal's office was introduced to General Grant by Mr. William G. Woodside, paymaster of the Baltimore and Ohio Railroad, as his private car sat on Howard Street waiting for a team to pull it to President Street Station. The General and Mrs. Grant were en route to Philadelphia, having declined an invitation to attend Ford's Theatre with the President that same evening. The next day, Admiral David Porter's flagship the USS *Tristam* arrived from Hampton Roads, Virginia. His reception was cut short when news arrived that President Lincoln had been assassinated the night before.

The city's population, both Loyalist and Rebel alike, were overwhelmed with grief and fear of a bloody reprisal. The mayor ordered all saloons closed and most business was suspended throughout the city. Between 11 a.m. and 12 noon, church and fire bells began to toll a solemn reference to the President's passing. Although the entire police and military force in the city was put on alert, no disturbance like the ones that had exemplified Baltimore's behavior in the past was reported.[74]

There were many ties to the Lincoln assassination in Baltimore. Paine's arrest in March has already been discussed. John Wilkes Booth was a member of a family of famous actors from Belair, Maryland, that had performed in Baltimore at the Holliday Street Theater. John T. Ford was an owner of the theater in Baltimore and the Ford's Theatre in Washington where Lincoln was shot. A letter in Booth's trunk implicated Samuel B. Arnold in the plot. "Was business so important that you could not remain in Baltimore until I saw you?" Federal detectives soon traced Arnold down and he was sent to Baltimore on one of the Bay Line vessels. Lt. Colonel Woolley ordered Captain Smith to escort Samuel Arnold to Washington where he was eventually convicted as one of the conspirators. When Smith read the description of Secretary of State William Seward's attacker, Lewis Paine immediately came to mind. "Height 6 1/2 feet, black hair ... Broad shoulders, strong looking man ... vulgar." As soon as the connection with Paine was verified, Smith arrested all the occupants of No. 16 North Eutaw Street. Twenty-two men and women were taken into custody and interviewed. Only the members of the Brason family were detained and at a second interview Miss Maggie broke down and told all she knew about Paine being a member of Mosby's command and using the alias Powell. A final connection comes with the trial of the conspirators. The noted Baltimore lawyer Reverdy Johnson was one of Mary Surratt's defense attorneys, and General Lew Wallace was a member of the military commission that tried her.[75]

The last great event in Baltimore's Civil War history was the passage of Lincoln's funeral train through the city on April 21, 1865. Lincoln's body laid in state at the Capitol Building for two days after his official funeral which fell on of all dates, April 19.

On Friday at 8:01 a.m., the funeral train left the Washington station to begin a journey that would carry the slain President along a route that was a reversal of his path from Springfield to the White House in 1861. The train consisted of a Baltimore and Ohio locomotive and tender, eight passenger cars, the funeral car, and a baggage car.

The locomotive was bedecked with black bunting and flags. On the front of the engine just above the cowcatcher was a framed portrait of Lincoln. In the funeral car were two coffins. The President's was a massive structure made of walnut and lined with lead. The outside was covered with broadcloth and had four silver handles on each side. On the lid was a silver plaque that identified its occupant:

"Abraham Lincoln
16th President of the United States
Born February 12, 1809
Died April 15, 1865"

The other contained the Lincolns' twelve-year-old son, Willie, who had died three years earlier. Mrs. Lincoln had ordered that the boy's body be exhumed and returned to Springfield with his father.[76]

The funeral train carried over 300 relatives and official mourners including President John Garrett of the Baltimore and Ohio Railroad, Rear Admiral Charles H. Davis representing the Secretary of the Navy, Brigadier General Edward D. Towson representing the Secretary of War, Lincoln's friend Ward Hill Lamon, and various members of the House and Senate. Moving ahead of the funeral train was a pilot engine to ensure safe passage to Camden Street Station.

The train arrived in Baltimore just before 10 o'clock in the morning. Lincoln's final visit to the city would last only four hours. Unfortunately for those standing in the pouring rain waiting to view the body, most of the time would be taken up with an elaborate procession. A detail of sergeants from the Veterans Corps removed the coffin from the train and placed it in a hearse made of rosewood with three-quarter inch plate glass windows. Inside was a newly invented system of springs that ensured a smooth ride for the coffin and its occupant. The hearse was pulled by four horses, each wearing black plumes upon their heads. Moving to the measured beat of the "Death March" punctuated with the firing salute of minute guns and the tolling of the city's church bells, the funeral procession took three hours as it passed along Eutaw, Baltimore, Gay, Chew, and Caroline Streets before arriving at the Merchant's Exchange on Market Street. Never in the history of Baltimore, or the nation, was any funeral procession in its long passage to Springfield, met with such an outpouring of universal grief. The great mercantile houses along the route were draped with the national flag, covered in endless streams of black mourning cloth. The following was printed on the front page of The Baltimore *American* the day after the funeral and attests to the enormity of the event.

"The Procession
Platoon of City Police,
Police Marshals Carmichael and Manly.
Colonel John Woolley, Chief Marshal.
Brigadier General Lockwood,
Commander of Escort and Staff.
Battery of Pennsylvania Artillery
Detachment of United States Marines,
Band.
Regiment of the Veteran Reserve Corps,
Band.
Infantry Troops of the First Brigade,
Band.
Infantry Troops of the Third Brigade,
Band.
Detachment of Wounded Colored Soldiers,
Squadron of Cavalry.
Staff Officers of Generals Wallace, Tyler and Kenly,
(All mounted)
Major General Lew Wallace,
With Brig. Gens. John R. Kenly; and E.B. Tyler,
Mounted Orderlies.
Band of the 2nd United States Artillery.

The Remains

(Following the coffin, in carriages, were the)
Pall Bearers from Washington;
Mourners and Committee of Senate and House of Representatives.
Officers of the Marine Corps and Navy.
Officers of the Army.
(The civic portion of the procession here commenced,
and was in the following order)
General J.S. Berry,
Marshal on the part of the State of Maryland.

J.Q.A. Herring,
Marshal on the part of the City of Baltimore.
Major R.S. King and Isaac Coale, Jr., Aides.
Governor Bradford and Lieutenant Governor Cox.
Honorable Thomas Swann, Governor elect;
State Comptroller, Secretary of State, and State Treasurer,
Other Officers of the State Government.
Staff Officers of Governor Bradford.
Band.
His Honor Mayor Chapman;
The Members of the City Council and other Municipal Officers.
A Military Detachment.
The Presbyterian Clergymen of the City, among whom
were Rev. Messrs. Hays, Sewall, Dunning, Stork, Wilson, McCauley,
Leakin and McKendree Reiley.
The Aged Guard of 1862,
Captain Samuel Childs, Marshal.
The Independent Greys, Company A,
Captain Stephen W. Jones;
Band.
The Union Club of Baltimore,
Thomas H. Morris, Marshal; Washington Booth and
George Small, Assistants.
Catholic Clergymen of the City, among whom were
Rev. Messrs. Dolan, Doughtery, Myers, Conkery and King.
Brothers of the Christian (Catholic) Schools, about fifty in number.
Band.
The East Baltimore Union League,
Captain James D. McKean, Marshal, 300 members.
The Signal Union Leaque,
Dr. Andrew Schwartz, Marshal.
The Washington Union Leaque,
Charles A. Davis, Marshal, with Captain Minnick's Band.
The Clerks and other Employees of the
Quartermaster's Department,
William S. Crowley, Marshal.
The Federal Officeholders in this City,
Charles Safell, Marshal.
The German Society.
The Baltimore City Fire Department,
headed by the Fire Commissioners, Chief and Assistant Engineers.

Independence Lodge No. 77, Independent Order of Odd Fellows,
Jacob H. Piercy, Marshal.
The Officers and Delegation of the Mechanical Monumental,
William Tell, Liberty, Schiller and Jackson Lodges, I.O.O.F.
The Grand Lodge of the State of Maryland,
with the Grand Officers.
The Topographical Union No. 12, of Baltimore,
C.S. Foster, Marshal.
Band.
The Great Council of the Improved Order of Red Men,
Robert D. Owens, Marshal.
The Journeymen Caulkers' Association,
Samuel D. Webb, Marshal.
The Social Turner's Union, and German Union Association,
C.H. Becker, Marshal, About 140 members in line, with
Captain Leinhardt's Band.
The German Singing Associations, composed of the
Leiderlantz, Arion Turner Liedertafel, Harmony, Germania
Mannechor, Arbeiter, Geeong Verein, Sangerchor, and
Baltimore Gassang Verein,
Under the Marshalship of John Hammetter.
Hebrew Literary Associations, comprising the
Mendelsshon, Cholophic, Independent and Mornic,
E. Goldman, Marshal.
The Oheb Shalom Congregation of Hanover Street,
The Colored Association,
George A. Hackett, Chief Marshal.
The Annual Conference of the African Methodist
Episcopal Church and Colored Clergy.
Delegates from the First Colored Christian
Commission of Baltimore.
The D.A. Payne Lodge of Samaritans.
The Grand Order of Nazaritee,
headed by Noah Butler.
The Grand Council and Subordinate Lodges of the Colored
Independent Order of Odd Fellows.
The Blue Lodge of Ancient York Masons.
The Masonic Grand Lodge of United States and Canadas.
The rear of the procession was brought up by a
large number of colored men,
who wore badges of mourning, &c."

*A*t The Exchange 10,000 people viewed the body in the scant hour the coffin was open. At 2:00 p.m. it was returned to the hearse and carried to the Northern Central Railroad Station where a locomotive from that line waited to pull the funeral train to Harrisburg. At the state line Governor Andrew Curtin boarded the train for the duration of its travel through the state of Pennsylvania. From Harrisburg it would pass through Philadelphia, New York, Albany, Buffalo, Columbus, Indianapolis, and Chicago before arriving in Springfield — a distance of 1,700 miles traveled on eight railroads. Lincoln's body was finally laid to rest on May 4 with his son Willie.[77]

In time the city recovered from the depression of Lincoln's funeral and turned to the more joyous occasion of the thousands of soldiers returning home. Federal regiments from Maryland were welcomed with official ceremonies. Veterans of the Confederate army simply made their way home as best they could for a private, but non the less sincere, reception. The Maryland Brigade returned to Camp Carroll the first week of June. Having been in combat from the Wilderness to Appomattox, they were anxious for their final discharge and rioted on June 6. General Wallace ordered General Lockwood to take command of the camp and sent the Eleventh Maryland and all available cavalry to quell the disturbance. About forty men were arrested and the perimeter of the camp heavily patrolled that night. This incident was the exception rather than the rule. For the most part veterans of both armies simply returned to the lives they had left at the time of their enlistment and viewed their former adversaries with respect rather than animosity for what they had accomplished on the battlefield.[78]

The federal government maintained a military presence in Baltimore City during the summer and winter of 1865. On February 1, 1866, Colonel Woolley received orders to close the provost marshal's office in Baltimore and report to the adjutant general in Washington. In recognition of his service in the Middle Department, Colonel Woolley was made a brevet brigadier general and Captain Smith, his chief detective, was brevetted a major.[79]

Throughout the balance of 1865, citizens of Baltimore returned from both official and self-imposed exile. The business community began its conversion back to a peacetime economy. The trading firm of Alex Brown and Sons, first established in 1800, had closed its Baltimore operation in 1862 due to the loss of business with its Southern customers. It reopened in 1865 and immediately began to reestablish old contacts in the Southern states as well as around the world. Baltimore, undamaged by war, remained an industrial city between North and South. It would

4-19

Typical scene of Union soldiers returning home. The Maryland Brigade returned to Camp Carroll the first week of June, 1865.

lead the way in the rehabilitation of the South in both commercial ventures and charitable undertakings. In April of 1866 the Ladies Southern Relief Association of Maryland held a fair in the Maryland Institute Hall, the same location as the Sanitary Fair of 1864. Using the Union Fair as

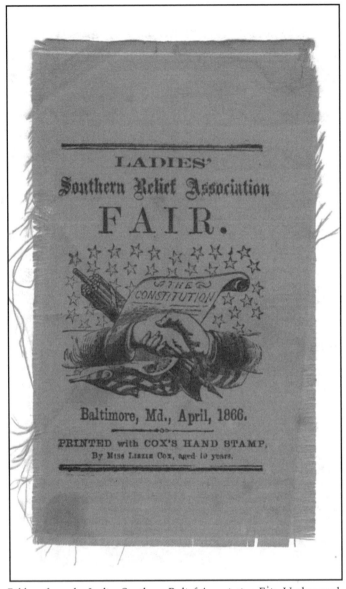

LADIES'

Southern Relief Association

FAIR.

THE
CONSTITUTION

Baltimore, Md., April, 1866.

PRINTED with COX'S HAND STAMP,
By Miss Lizzie Cox, aged 10 years.

Ribbon from the Ladies Southern Relief Association Fair: Undamaged by war, Baltimore led the way in aiding the South.

a model, they were able to raise over $160,000.00. The money was disbursed throughout the Southern states with a considerable portion going to the residents of the Shenandoah Valley which Sheridan had so efficiently laid waste to in the closing months of the war. Baltimore's postwar generosity was long remembered in the South.[80]

REPORT

OF THE

LADIES'

ASSOCIATION

OF MARYLAND.

SEPTEMBER 1st, 1866.

BALTIMORE:

PRINTED BY KELLY & PIET,

174 BALTIMORE STREET.

1866

Report of the Southern Relief Association: The ladies raised $160,000 to aid the South.

(National Park Service)

Fort McHenry before the war.

V

Fort McHenry

*B*eginning in 1841, several graduates of the U. S. Military Academy served their first tours of duty at Fort McHenry. Second Lieutenant John F. Reynolds was assigned here from 1841 to 1842. He would fall on the first day of Gettysburg. Second Lieutenant Abner Doubleday served two tours — from 1844-1845 and 1850-1852. It was Doubleday that fired the first shot from Fort Sumter in 1861. First Lieutenant Edward Otho C. Ord served from 1844-1846. As commander of the Nineteenth Corps he would pursue Lee to Appomatox Court House in 1865. Major William H. French and Company K, First U.S. Artillery served from 1855 until June 9, 1859, when they departed for Fort Clark, Texas, leaving Ordnance Sergeant Thomas Dailey in command.[1]

Dailey was described as "a trustworthy, industrious, faithful old soldier" whose responsibility it became, with three laborers, to safeguard the fort and grounds. For eighteen months Dailey remained in command, until the arrival on January 15, 1861, of Co. I, First U.S. Artillery under Captain Joseph A. Haskins from the Baton Rouge Arsenal, Louisiana. Five days earlier he had been forced to surrender the federal arsenal under a superior force led by the governor of Louisiana. Haskins' command remained at Fort McHenry until February 2 when they were ordered to Washington.[2]

Other federal forces temporarily garrisoned the fort; First Lt. Andrew J. Hays and thirty U.S. Marines from the Washington Navy Yard (Jan. 9-Feb. 2); Colonel Horace H. Brooks, Co "H" Second U.S. Artillery (Jan. 15-Feb. 1); and First Lt. Samuel H. Reynolds, Co. "C" First U.S. Infantry (Feb. 1-26).[3]

On February 26, 1861, the command of Fort McHenry was entrusted to Captain John Cleveland Robinson, a veteran of the Mexican and Seminole Wars. Robinson and Company B, Fifth U.S. Infantry found garrison life routine and uneventful. This situation was altered in April by the determination of Baltimore's citizens "to resist at every hazard the passage of [Northern] troops through the city." The Baltimore *American* went so far as to state "that Baltimore is to be the battlefield of the southern revolution."[4]

The historic past was not lost upon the citizens of Baltimore. Similar events, against the British army on April 19, 1775, had started the fight for American Independence. Now, eighty-six years later, the country was unknowingly about to enter a Civil War that would change forever the landscape and conscience of America. For Captain Robinson, the coming fury of the Civil War would lead him, in time, to a place called Oak Knoll at Gettysburg in 1863.

Following the capitulation of Fort Sumter in April of 1861, only four major coastal fortifications remained in the hands of the federal government: Fort Taylor and the navy base at Key West and Fort Pickens at Pensacola; Fortress Monroe in Virginia at Hampton Roads; and Forts Carroll and McHenry in Baltimore harbor. On April 18, Robinson's command was relieved by Company I, Second U.S. Artillery, that remained the permanent garrison throughout the war.[5]

As seceding states began to appropriate federal installations throughout the South, Fort McHenry became a primary concern for the military officials in Washington. The garrison was reinforced during the summer of 1861 by companies of the First, Second, and Fourth U.S. Artillery and by various state regiments throughout the war.[6]

Although the fort never witnessed actual conflict, Fort McHenry's role during the Civil War was far from insignificant. It stood ready to repel a naval attack had the South possessed the ships to do so. During the turbulent days following the Pratt Street Riot, its guns and troops curbed the ardor of secessionists in the city and provided a rallying point for Unionists throughout the state. As the foundation of Baltimore's defense system, Fort McHenry also became a major depot for prisoners of war. The same railroads that brought products to the port in peacetime were utilized to carry Rebel prisoners from the battlefields of Antietam, Gettysburg, and the war in the West. In the next four years, Baltimore and Fort McHenry would provide the federal government a keystone in the preservation of not only the capital, but as the center for communications, supplies and troop embarkation to the various theaters of war.

For many historians and citizens who live within the Monumental City, Fort McHenry has remained the center of the story of Baltimore during the Civil War. The story of this nineteenth century landmark of American history has been condensed into four categories to provide a brief narrative of its role during the war: Armament, Prisoners of War, Military Executions, and Garrison Life.

ARMAMENT

*I*n 1839, twenty-four years after the War of 1812 had ended, the army began a modernization program to upgrade the seacoast armament of Fort McHenry, even as preliminary drawings were being made for a newer fortification four miles below at Sollers Shoals to be called Fort Carroll. The fifty pieces of ordnance, of 24, 32, and 42 caliber, were mounted on wooden carriages to replace the guns that had successfully defended the fort in 1814.

In 1857, a lighter piece designed for field service, the 12-Pounder Napoleon Field Gun, Model 1857, was rapidly being manufactured to meet the needs of the federal government. Developed in France in the 1850's, this smoothbore weapon, capable of firing shot, shell, case shot and canister, became, for its maneuverability and effectiveness, the most popular field gun of the war. The first field tests conducted in the United States were made at Fort McHenry in May 1857, by Major Alfred Mordecai, chief ordnance officer for the War Department.[7]

The movement of artillery through Baltimore in the early summer of 1861 attracted the attentiveness of Southerners who were looking with a

Fifty pieces of ordnance were mounted on wooden carriages.

wary eye towards the federal build-up in the city and Fort McHenry. On May 26, 1861, two 10-inch, Model 1844 Columbiads, also cast at Pittsburgh, arrived in the city, destined for Fort McHenry. One of these, while waiting downtown, was found to be spiked by unknown personages in the "unwarrantable act" to prevent their use by the government. The obstructions were removed, and they were conveyed to Fort McHenry and mounted — facing Baltimore. These two columbiads remained the largest of Fort McHenry's armament throughout the war.[8]

By 1861, the seacoast guns, perfected in the post War of 1812 era, were becoming obsolete, as metallurgic technology had perfected a new powerful seacoast armament, designed by Captain Thomas J. Rodman, capable of hurtling a 400 pound solid shot three miles. The Rodman Gun, whose massive smoothbore calibers measured 8-inch, 10-inch and even 15-inches were cast at the Fort Pitt Foundry in Pittsburgh, the West Point Foundry in New York, and at the South Boston Foundry.

On May 27, a 15-inch Rodman Gun, christened the "Lincoln Gun," destined for Fort Monroe, Virginia, arrived at the Northern Central Depot on Calvert Street. It was the largest gun yet manufactured at the Fort Pitt Foundry, Pittsburgh, Pennsylvania, cast on December 23, 1860, by Knap, Rudd and Company. The range of the gun had been recorded at 5,730 yards with a 320 pound shell. It was placed on a two-wheeled wagon and drawn by oxen through the streets to Locust Point to await its eventual shipment.

A few days later on June 1, another Rodman Gun, known as the "Union Gun," cast with a 12-inch bore and rifled, arrived in Baltimore and taken to Locust Point under guard of a company of Pennsylvania volunteers. While being loaded on the schooner *J.J. Baril* on June 7, for conveyance to Fort Monroe, it went overboard and sank to the bottom of the harbor. After the laborious task of retrieving the 52, 005 pound tube it continued its journey, arriving at Monroe the following month.[9]

By July 1861, a total of seventy-six cannon and mortars were mounted at Fort McHenry. A New York Times correspondent visiting the fort described its armament as follows:

> "Fresh guns have been mounted, and I observe that all mortars and a part of the Columbiads on the landward side [towards the city] are kept loaded — in preparation for any emergency ... Fort McHenry is about two miles from the centre of the city, and it is well understood that it could drop shells, hot or otherwise, into all the houses in the [secessionist] infected [Mount Vernon] district with the utmost ease. I trust the necessity for doing so may never arise.."[10]

On September 17, 1861, Lieutenant Colonel William Brewerton of the U.S. Army Corps of Engineers surveyed the existing ordnance at the fort and issued the following inventory to his commanding officer, Brigadier General Joseph G. Totten:

Bastion No. 1
1 8-inch S.C. Howitzer
1 42 Pdr.
1 12 Pdr. Brass Mountain Howitzer
1 8-inch Siege Mortar
1 10-inch Columbiad*

Bastion No. 2
2 24 Pdr.
1 10-inch Siege Mortar*

Bastion No. 3
1 10-inch Columbiad*
1 6 Pdr. Brass Field Gun
1 24 Pdr.

Bastion No. 4
2 24 Pdr.
1 12 Pdr. Brass Field Howitzer*
1 10-inch Sea Coast Mortar

Bastion No. 5
1 24 Pdr.
1 6 Pdr. Brass Field Gun
1 10-inch Sea Coast Mortar*

Mounted on the terreplein between Bastions Nos. 1-2
3 10-inch S.C. Mortars*

On terreplein between Bastions Nos. 1-3
2 10-inch S.C. Mortars
1 24 Pdr.

Mounted in the dry moat between Bastions Nos. 1-2
3 10-inch S.C. Mortars*

Outer Battery [facing the harbor]
2 8-inch S.C. Howitzers
18 42 Pdrs.
14 32 Pdrs.
7 24 Pdrs.

Ravelin
3 8-inch S.C. Howitzer
4 32 Pdrs.

Parade Ground [inside fort]
1 6 Pdr. Brass Field Gun

Dismounted Ordnance [The following ordnance was supplied with carriages, etc., and were ready for mounting. They were placed on wooden skids on the glacis between Bastions Nos. 1-2 along the road to the fort.]

1 8-inch S.C. Howitzer
14 32 Pdrs.
11 24 Pdrs.
[* denotes armament facing towards Baltimore][11]

In all, seventy-six mortars and cannon stood ready to defend the fort of which two 10-inch columbiads and five 10-inch siege mortars were positioned to fire on the city that McHenry was originally built to protect, a fact not lost by the veteran "Old Defenders" that had saved the city in 1814. Nor had it been lost on General Dix who remarked in a report dated August 12, when he "was not quite satisfied with Fort McHenry. It is very strong on the water side, but, like most of our harbor fortifications, was constructed with no special reference to attack by land."[12]

One of the most pressing problems to be remedied that summer was the inadequate facilities for the storage of the increased amounts of gun powder being shipped to the fort, from the E.I. Du Pont & Company in Wilmington, Delaware. Alterations were made to the old 1814 personnel bombproof casemates (each measuring 18' x 30') located on either side of Sally Port, capable of storing 20,000 pounds of powder. The location of such large quantities in a vulnerable site, the only throughfare into the star fort, prompted an officer to note the potential threat to this "common throughfare, with people passing all the time, [and] men smoking."[13]

In 1863, the War Department authorized the construction of a brick-vaulted detached powder magazine to hold the increased shipments of powder to Fort McHenry. By April 1864, the magazine was completed, capable of securing 1,500 barrels of powder.

By 1865, preparations were underway to replace Fort McHenry's seaward mounted guns with the newer 8-inch, 10-inch and 15-inch

Rodmans, that had been authorized in 1861 to replace the pre-war sea-coast ordnance, a modification initially completed at Fort McHenry by the summer of 1866.

PRISONERS OF WAR

On October 7, 1861, Lt. Colonel William Hoffman was made Commissary General of Prisoners for the federal government, a post he held throughout the war. He established rules and an elaborate system of inspections and reports that were issued to the twenty-three prisons that had been erected by the end of the war, compared to thirteen in 1861.

To identify the various prisons used as federal prisons during the war is useful since many prisoners brought to Baltimore were only temporarily detained at Fort McHenry. Early in the war, federal fortifications like Fort McHenry were utilized since garrisons provided a quick and temporary solution. Later as the number of prisoners of war increased, more permanent sites were created from existing buildings on site, such as the federal hospital at Point Lookout, Maryland, while others were large stockade enclosures with tents and hastily erected buildings, such as Johnson's Island, Ohio. The sites listed below were used for many prisoners, soldier and citizens alike, who were transferred from Fort McHenry.

Site	Location
Fort Delaware	Delaware River, Delaware
Point Lookout	St. Mary's County, Maryland
Fort Lafayette	New York Harbor
Fort Warren	Boston, Massachusetts
Johnson's Island	Sandusky, Ohio
Old Capitol Prison	Washington, D.C.
Camp Parole	Annapolis, Maryland (Exchange site)
Fortress Monroe	Hampton Roads, Virginia (Exchange site)

Unlike other federal prisons, Fort McHenry's prisoners were temporarily held until transportation to more permanent sites could be arranged. The fort's recorded mortality rate lists only 28 prisoners of war had died out of the 15,091 who were detained here from March 1863 to June 1865. For the period 1861-62 less than 10 deaths were recorded.

The small number may have resulted from the medical facilities established in Baltimore as well as their temporary detainment.[14]

With rail connections to Baltimore, especially from the western campaigns, prisoners were brought directly to the B&O Camden Street and Northern Central Depots and thence marched the three miles to Fort McHenry. Upon arrival, each prisoner's name, date of capture or arrest, date of confinement, regiment or residence, and prisoner deposition remarks were recorded.

In a report for Colonel William Hoffman dated September 14, 1863, the commander of Fort McHenry, General William Morris, divided the prisoners into three classes. The following are examples obtained from Fort McHenry's "Registry of Prisoners."

"First. Soldier prisoners, or those belonging to the U.S. Army and charged with offenses punishable by military law."[15]

The following federal soldiers were confined at Fort McHenry in the winter of 1862.

David Scofield
6th NY Artillery   12/01/1862   Sleeping on post

Adam Clark
13th PA Cavalry   11/12/1862   Deserter

James Thompson
6th NY Artillery   12/18/1862   Impertinence to chaplain

James Wallace
3rd New York   11/14/1862   Recruiting the enemy[16]

"Second. Prisoners of war, who are subject to no punishment except that of being held in safe confinement until duly exchanged."[17]

Henry Hall Brogden
Acting Adjutant — C.S.A. Signal Corps.

A native Marylander, Brogden was captured carrying dispatches on May 3, 1863, near the mouth of the Patuxent River by a federal gunboat. Taken to Point Lookout, he was sent to Fort McHenry and imprisoned there on May 7. He wrote of his confinement within the south wing of the Sally Port prisons:

"The cell in which I was confined was three feet wide by six feet long, but was ten or twelve feet high. It was under the parapet in the [south wing of the sally port prison] casement ... There was no window and no means of ventilation. It lay at the upper end of a narrow passageway [2' x 10'] on which two other cells opened. The passage was entered through a small door at the lower end from the guard room ... There was a grated iron door, which was closed all day, and there was a solid wooden door which was closed when the flag fell in the evening, and opened at guard mount in the morning. There was no bedstead or chair, their being no room for such luxuries. I was allowed a mattress, which I placed on the damp floor at night, and stood up on end against the wall in the day. I was not allowed bed linen. At no time were the walls of my cell dry, the rear wall particularly. Moisture trickled down it the whole time and could fill my hand with a green slime simply by passing it up the face of the wall. I was not allowed knife and fork, my food being cut up by the sentinel outside and pushed through the grated door while I held a tin plate to catch it. I do not remember that the plate was washed during the entire time of my imprisonment in the cell. A tin basin, filled with water, was brought into the cell when the cleaning (so called) was done each morning about eight o'clock, but there was no towel ..." [18]

On June 29, Mr. Brogden was briefly sent to Fort Delaware during the Gettysburg campaign and later returned on August 2 and subsequently on December 10, sent to Fortress Monroe for exchange.

"Third. Political prisoners, or those other than the first class who are charged with offenses for which they may be tried and punished by a court-martial or military commission"[19]

On April 27, 1861, with the suspension of the writ of habeas corpus, federal officers began to arrest citizens who were suspected of treason, blockade runners, impeding the passage of Union troops, Confederate sympathizers, and printing secessionist materials.

Those arrested included individuals who committed or were accused of hostilities without being part of any organized hostile army. From May 1861 to February 17, 1862, one hundred and twenty-five political arrests were made. Of these, twenty-nine were arrests for disloyalty by members of the Maryland Legislature.[20]

In the period from September 14, 1861 to August 15, 1862, seventeen Baltimore newspaper owners and editors were arrested and confined at Fort McHenry, their papers suspended. Most notably those papers suppressed were The *Catholic Mirror*, *The South*, and The *Daily Exchange*, all declared by the postmaster general as "open disunionists," also noting that "*The* [Baltimore] *Sun* is sympathetic [to the South], but less diabolical."[21]

On February 14, 1862, Lincoln transferred the jurisdiction of all political prisoners held under the State Department, to the War Department. From January 1863 to July 1865 a total of 2,094 political prisoners were detained at Fort McHenry. [22]

Political prisoners were afforded more leisure accommodations within the old quarters of the star fort, separated from the "more vesicle class of offenders" who were held within the confinement cells of the south wing of the Sally Port prisons and the large stockade wall enclosure of the provost prison outside the fort.

During the war, the following Oath of Allegiance was presented to employees of the city of Baltimore, such as James Hall, a fireman with Engine Company No. 4 on August 15, 1864. A similar oath was administered by federal officials to Confederate soldiers, prisoners of the State Department — political prisoners.

I, *James Hall*

Do solemnly swear that I will bear true allegiance to the UNITED STATES, and support and sustain the CONSTITUTION and laws thereof; that I will maintain the national sovereignty paramount to that of all State, County, or Corporate powers; that I will discourage, discountenance, and forever oppose *Secession, Rebellion* and the disintegration of the FEDERAL UNION; that I disclaim and denounce all faith and fellowship with the so-called *Confederate States* and *Confederate Armies*, and pledge my property and my life to the sacred performance of this my solemn oath of allegiance to the Government of the UNITED STATES. So help me God.

Sworn and Subscribed before me, a Justice of the Peace in and for the City of Baltimore, State of Maryland, on this *fifteenth* day of *August* eighteen hundred and sixty *four* .

[Signed Justice of the Peace][23]

George McCaffray
Suspected of treason and imprisoned from April 26-
August 7 1862.

Among the many civilians held at Fort McHenry was George McCaffray, a Baltimore City resident, arrested on April 26, 1862, for "refusing to take the oath of allegiance." He was imprisoned in the north wing Sally Port prison within the star fort. In a letter to his wife Sue, dated July 27, Mr. McCaffray commented:

> "When I left you on Tuesday you know I was quite sick & feverish, the confinement in the cell did not improve it. About half past seven the door was shut & the heat was awful, think of it seven of us in a cell about thirteen feet square, but Gen'l Morris said he had no other room. I shall never forget that night. I was in a high fever raving all night, walking in the sun so much after my sickness no doubt produced it. If I had been some guilty wench that night's suffering would be sufficient punishment. The next night one more prisoner was added & I was preparing for another night of suffering when Gen'l Morris came to the door and called out two others and myself and told us we could occupy the tent in front of our cell, anything I thought is preferable to sleeping again in that cell, so we went there and I slept tolerably well. In the morning however our bed covers were quite wet with the dew .... I would like you to lend me some old tin bucket you are not using. A small one will do to keep drinking water in as we can get none here. I have seen Henry McCaffray but not to speak to him. He now occupies my old quarters...."[24]

Mr. McCaffray was released on August 7 with his brother upon taking the oath. Henry McCaffray (George's brother), a music dealer was arrested July 24 for "publishing a piece of music entitled "Stonewall Quickstep," dedicated to General T[homas] J. Jackson, C.S.A."[25]

Mrs. Maria Coe
"A notorious spy and rebel mail carrier" confined on March 7, 1863.

One of the three known women who were held briefly at Fort McHenry was Maria Coe, captured in Loudon County, Virginia. She warranted a note in the "Guard Registry" upon her arrival:

"This woman is a most notorious spy and rebel mail carrier. She recruited with her sister Mrs. Foy where rebel mails are made up. She generally goes ahead of the Rebels on horseback to see if the federals are around and [then] conveys news back to the rebels and pilots them through the country .... She is a very dangerous woman and has done a great deal of damage [and] is also concerned in smuggling goods into Rebel lines..."[26]

Mrs. Coe was questioned by General Morris and released the same day to the care of the Provost Marshal's Office in Baltimore. Her final disposition is unknown.

The Provost Prison

*T*he primary prison facilities at Fort McHenry were located outside the main star fort upon the east grounds, near the east seawall and conveniently accessible to the docks. The prisons consisted of three two-story brick stables originally built in 1843 by Captain Samuel Ringgold's artillery corps. In September 1862, the stables were converted to temporary prisons. In fact, as the prisoners arrived in one door, the horses went out another, such was the haste in preparing accommodations for the new tenants of "Hotel McHenry."

Each building measured 120' x 30' and was divided into four rooms, two above and two below. Two of the former stables were surrounded by a high stockade fence approximately 25' high with a parapet walkway complete with sentry watch boxes. The third stable continued to function as a stable for officers until converted in 1863 as more facilities were needed.

Within the enclosure, each prison room and adjacent yard was assigned to a class of prisoners; Confederate officers, enlisted men, Union bounty jumpers, and one room for Negroes that were brought in with Confederate soldiers. The yards provided an exercise area for various recreational activities, meals and roll call.[27]

For the prisoners detained here, life was a daily routine controlled by guards and the close confines of the adjacent prison yards. Their confinement was made more difficult by the humid summer days and, perhaps worse for a Southern soldier, the cold winter nights. The availability of rare prisoner diaries and federal records provide sufficient data to reconstruct a brief outline of prison life at Fort McHenry for the common Confederate prisoner of war.

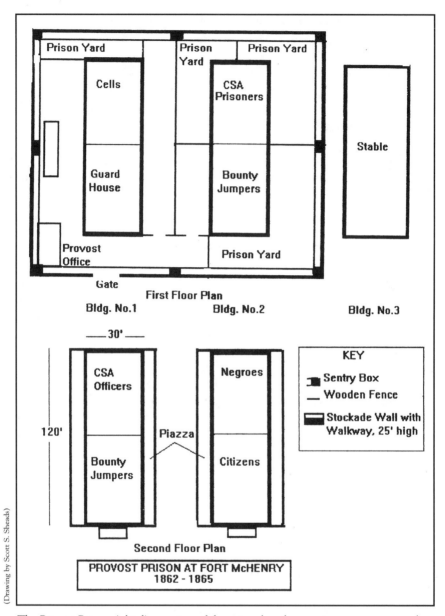

The Provost Prison: A bird's eye view of the prison based on contemporary maps and diaries.

Private William Marshall, C.S.A., wounded at the Battle of Antietam in September 1862 and treated at the National Hotel hospital on Camden Street was confined in the provost prison at Fort McHenry on January 25, 1863.

Private William Marshall
Brooks Artillery, C.S.A.

"On Tuesday evening we were conveyed under escort to this memorable den. Imagine our feelings after such lavish kindness, nursing, and petting as we have had from the ladies of Shepherdstown [,West Virginia], and now having to submit to the gross indignity of living in a filthy, crowded horse stable — forty rebels occupying the space for twelve horses....." Rats were everywhere. "Their roving, predatory excursions have caused our haversacks to suffer immensely ... Most of last night I stood sentry armed with a crutch, while our party slumbered....A bitter snowstorm raged all yesterday and has not subsided. Notwithstanding, two heroic ladies visited us and consoled us very much, and although the mean, suspecting bluebacks watch them like cats after mice during the interview, they make nothing by the operation — those hoops are grand in an emergency!....It's uncertain when we leave this garden of roses...."[28]

On January 31, Marshall was sent to Fort Monroe, Virginia for exchange.[29]

Reverend T.D. Witherspoon
Forty-Second Mississippi Regiment

Witherspoon, a Confederate officer who was captured at Gettysburg, was confined on July 22, 1863, at "Hotel Fort McHenry." The stable (prison) loft in which he was detained, was above the stable still being used for Union officer's horses.

"The floor, which separated us from our neighing neighbors beneath us, was full of broad seams from the shrinkage of boards of which it was composed, so that the hot, steamy air from below had full access to us, and during the oppressive days and sultry nights of July and August, with the thin roof of shingles between us and the sun, and the hot steam arising from the stalls beneath, our situation was anything but comfortable....On either side of the long apartment rooms were rows of two story berths (or bunks in soldier parlance), made of rough boards, without mattresses, or straw or bedding of any kind, our only protection from the hard board being found in the army blanket, which each prisoner had brought with him to the fort, or with which he had been provided through the generosity of friends..."[30]

Rations — Daily rations issued by the post commissary for prisoners consisted of pork, fresh or salted beef, flour or hard bread, beans, molasses, rice, coffee, vinegar, onion, salt and pepper. In addition fresh vegetables from sympathetic citizens were left at the outer gate — hopeful of their delivery. Political prisoners held within the confines of the Star Fort were often the fortunate recipients of delicacies brought directly to them from family members and friends.

An abstract of provisions issued in November 1863 by the post commissary for 256 prisoners of war, including political prisoners, gives an idea of the large quantity of rations that were distributed each month at Fort McHenry:

2967 rations of pork	2480 rations of fresh beef
2529 rations of salt beef	1861 rations of onions
7587 rations of hard bread	6215 rations of rice
7830 rations of beans	7976 rations of potatoes
7976 rations of coffee	7976 rations of sugar
7976 rations of vinegar	7976 rations of salt
383 rations of flour	7976 rations of adamantine candles
7976 rations of soap	389 rations of molasses
7976 rations of pepper[31]	

For those held within the stockade, twice a day, a large camp kettle containing 30-40 gallons of coffee, and borne on a pole held by orderlies, was served every morning and evening, with a quart of bean soup at noon. A smaller camp kettle delivered daily contained meat or "salt horse" (army name for pickled beef), the next day, pork. To the above rations, Irish potatoes were served once a week. One prisoner remembered that, "None of us had any cups at first, and, as I saw I was about to lose my soup, I grabbed up my old hat and, by sinking in the crown from the outside, I made a depression large enough to hold my soup, and, soaking my bread in it, ate it that way."[32]

Recreational Activities — The melancholy routine of prison life gave birth to a variety of expedients by prisoners to enlighten their imprisonment. Besides the usual and more civilized literary and debating societies that flourished, were the highlights of those with less than intellectual pursuits to pass the time. Here are a few:

The Department of the Patapsco

Every morning, lookouts, chosen by their Confederate comrades, posted guard at one of the many subterranean holes where rats burrowed beneath the prison walls and buildings. When the enemy was sighted, the alarm was sounded, and the chase was on by soldiers of the Department, to rid the prison of the enemy, or have them for sale, as an exotic compliment to the usual prison fare.[33]

The Lookout

The high wooden stockade walls surrounding the prison made it impossible for those within to view outside activities. To alleviate this, a high wooden post with a cross-piece platform on top was situated in the middle of the yard giving "the lookout" the opportunity to have "a fine view" of the outside world and convey the news to those below.[34]

Battlefield of the Ants

In one of the prison yards there was an ant bed where prisoners would, by picking lice off their bodies, engage them upon the ants. The result was "a regular pitched battle." It was, as one prisoner remembered, "great sport for the prisoners."[35]

The Dress Parade

Every morning following the dress parade of the Union garrison, the prisoners had theirs. A prisoner would, in imitation of a drum-major with his ceremonial baton, mark time with his own band as they paraded along the line of prisoners. "He moved up and down along the line of the regiment; followed by his band, one with a half flour-barrel suspended from his neck for a drum, another with two tin plates as cymbals, a third with an old cracked flageolet ... and the fourth with a course comb, covered with a slip of paper .. the scene was striking beyond description, especially when, as was generally the case, the full power of the orchestra was exhausted upon *Hail Columbia, Yankee Doodle,* or some other favorite National air." Afterwards a long string of orders for the day would be read in preparation for the duties that awaited them.[36]

"The Black Hole of Calcutta" — The most notorious of these provost prison rooms was what one prisoner called "the black hole of Calcutta." Seven cells were located on the first floor, each measuring "five feet wide by eight feet long, made of two-inch oak plank doubled, with a hole in each door ten inches square, with iron bars across, and ventilated holes opposite in the brick wall. The cold blew right in on us...." Wounded and captured at Gettysburg, Sergeant James T. Wells, Co. A, Second South Carolina Infantry recalled his experiences. "In the dark hole, on the first floor, were confined some of the most villainous cut-throats it has ever been my misfortune to meet. They were convicted of different crimes and had different terms to serve. All of them wore balls and chains, and they made night hideous with their curses, screams, and rattling of the chains."[37]

*A*lthough Fort McHenry's prison was probably not the worst, it certainly left an impressionable mark on many a Confederate soldier's memories. For Sergeant Wells and the Reverend Witherspoon, and thousands held here, confinement was temporary. Steamboats would arrive almost daily to transfer them to federal prisons at Fort Delaware and Point Lookout, two sites considered the Northern rivals to that of Andersonville, Georgia.

Throughout the war a series of orders in regards to prisoners were released by the President and the War Department. Here are a few of the most notable ones:[38]

April 27, 1861 Lincoln suspends the writ of habeas corpus between Philadelphia and Washington along the military railroad including Annapolis.

February 14, 1862 *Executive Order in relation to State Prisoners, No. 1*
State prisoners are transferred from the State Department to the War Department. The President also orders War Secretary Stanton to release all political prisoners who were willing to give parole and not to render aid or comfort to the enemies of the United States. Edwin M. Stanton, Secretary of War.

February 27, 1862 *"Executive Order No. 2, in relation to the State Prisoners"*
That a special commission of two persons, one military and one civilian be appointed to examine the cases of state prisoners, and to determine if they should be discharged or remain in military custody. Major-General John A. Dix of Baltimore and the Hon. Edwards Pierrepont, of New York were appointed. Edwin M. Stanton, Secretary of War.

July 17, 1862 Congressional act authorizes the President to extend a pardon and amnesty to persons in states in rebellion.

July 22, 1862 A prisoner exchange cartel agreement was reached with the Confederate States for the mutual exchange of prisoners.

August 8, 1862 *"Order to prevent evasion of military duty and for suppression of disloyal practices, and for the suspension of the writ of habeas corpus."* War Department suspends the writ of habeas corpus throughout the country. Edwin M. Stanton, Secretary of War.

August 8, 1862 War Department gave authority to US Marshals and Chiefs of Police to arrest and imprison any person who may be engaged by act, speech, or writing that gave aid or comfort to the enemy or any disloyal practice against the United States. Edwin M. Stanton, Secretary of War.

September 24, 1862 The President, by proclamation, suspends writ of habeas corpus for entire country. President of the United States and countersigned by William H. Seward, Secretary of State.

September 26, 1862 Authorized a Provost Marshal General for the War Department. It also appointed one or more marshals in each state to report to the Provost Marshal General, and to arrest all deserters and send them to the military authority.

November 22, 1862 *"Duplicity of the Secretary of War-Public Order for the Release of Prisoners of State-Private Order to Disregard the One Publicly Promulgated."* To discharge "all persons now in military custody."

November 24, 1862 11:50 a.m. A secret order was sent to all officers, commanding: "None of the prisoners confined at your post will be released under orders of the War Department of the 22nd Inst., without special instructions from the Department. By order of the Secretary of War." E.D. Townsend, A.A.G.

November 27, 1862 Maryland political prisoners at Fort Warren are ordered released by orders of the War Department.

December 8, 1862 All prisoners at Fort McHenry to be sent to Fort Monroe, Virginia

March 3, 1863 *"An Act Relating to Habeas Corpus, and Regulating Judicial Proceedings in Certain Cases."* Congress authorizes the President to suspend writ of habeas corpus through the "Habeas Corpus Indemnity Act."

June 17, 1863 The commander of Fort McHenry, General Morris announces "no persons will be permitted to visit prisoners."

October 10, 1863 Stanton orders postponement of further exchanges or paroles.

November 4, 1863 General Robert Schenck issues General Order No. 53 directing all provost marshals and unit commanders to arrest any persons suspected to be disloyal.

December 8, 1863 President offers a Proclamation of Amnesty and Reconstruction for a full pardon to all Confederates who would take the oath of allegiance (except CSA government officials and officers).

March 12, 1864 Fort Delaware is detached from the Middle Department and reports directly to the War Department.

April 17, 1864 General Grant orders no more prisoner exchanges.

May 29, 1865 President Andrew Johnson issues a general Amnesty Proclamation to all former Confederate soldiers.

Among the last prisoners held at Fort McHenry were six rebel officers who were captured on May 10, 1865, at Irwinsville, Georgia, while accompanying President Jefferson Davis and his family. Apprehended by Lt. Colonel B. Prichard, Fourth Michigan Cavalry, they were ordered confined at Fort McHenry by Rear-Admiral William Restford, USN. While President Davis was sent to Fort Monroe, the following party arrived at Fort McHenry on May 25, 1865.

> First Lieutenant Leland Hathaway, Fourteenth Kentucky Cavalry
> Midshipman Jeff L. Howell, C.S.N.
> Private John Messect, Second Kentucky Cavalry, Co. A
> Private William M. Monroe, Second Kentucky Cavalry, Co. A
> Major Vichi Maurand, Richardson's Virginia Artillery
> Captain Woody, Madison County Artillery

By July 26, 1865, all had been released.[39]

MILITARY EXECUTIONS

"Offenders against the law of nations. — These, accused of being spies, pirates, recruiting within our lines, under sentence of death, &c., occupy two rooms in the interior of the fort. Only a portion are in irons. The doors are open all day to admit air and light, and exercise in the interior parade is allowed for half an hour each day..."

P.A. Porter, Colonel, Eighth New York Heavy Artillery, Commanding Post in the absence of General William W. Morris, December 1863.[40]

At least five known soldiers or alleged Confederate spies were sentenced to be executed at Fort McHenry, but had their sentences commuted by the President. Three others were not so fortunate. The following affairs of military justice were dutifully recorded by *The Sun* and the fort's "Guard Registry."

William H. Rodgers, John B.H. Embert, Braxton Lynn, and Samuel B. Herne
Suspected of being Rebel spies and blockade runners, August 1864.
Privates in Co. B, First Maryland Infantry, CSA.[41]

Found guilty by a military commission on August 18, 1864, *The Baltimore Sun* reported that they were to be sentenced "to be hung between the hours of 5 and 8 o'clock on the morning of the 29th. The sentence has yet to be approved by the President." That morning, Private George W. Kimball, Fifth Massachusetts Regiment, then stationed at the fort, and a carpenter by trade, entered in his diary:

> "I had the machine [gallows] all ready for them & was disappointed in not seeing how it worked ... I put the ropes all up and we all supposed they would be hung but the President has seen fit to have their sentences changed to imprisonment. I think he shows to much leniency [sic] for I think if any one should be hung it is a spie [sic]."[42]

The gallows built in 1862 for one, was enlarged by Kimball to receive four. For Samuel B. Hearn and his compatriots, an unusual circumstance of a personal reprieve by the President came at an opportune moment. On the night of August 28, Mrs. John Gittings and several concerned citizens traveled to Washington to meet with the President with petitions for the men's pardon from the gallows. They found the President at his country retreat north of the capital at the "Soldiers' Home." Despite the late hour, Lincoln received the Baltimore delegation. When he learned that Mrs. Gittings was the woman who three years earlier, in February 1861, had befriended Mrs. Lincoln, prompted the President to issue a pardon for the three men on August 31. The men, reprieved of their fates, were sent on September 4 to the Albany Penitentiary in New York at hard labor until January 1865 when they were transferred to Fort Monroe, Virginia, where a parole was subsequently issued.[43]

Private Joseph Kuhne
Co. F, Second Maryland Regiment, U.S.A.
Arrested for murder and executed March 7, 1862

On this crisp clear morning carpenters erected a wooden scaffold outside the Star Fort on the parade grounds. Upon its completion, a black walnut coffin was placed beneath it. Nearly 4,000 federal troops arrived "to the sound of martial music and the heavy tread of soldiery." From all quarters within Baltimore they came to witness the grim display of a military execution — the first ever at Fort McHenry. Kuhne had been found guilty for the murder of his Second Lieutenant, J. Davis Whitson, on September 10, 1861. *The Sun* reported the execution:

"At noon all the military had reached the parade ground at Fort McHenry and formed a hollow square within the enclosure. The gallows was erected near the centre of the ground and presented to the beholder a fearful sign of recompense for violating the laws of God and men by depriving another of life. Thousands of citizens had congregated outside the enclosure, but a strong guard prevented them from advancing nearer to the scene of execution. Shortly after twelve o'clock there emerged a wagon from the gateway of the fort guarded by a strong military force. The condemned man was in the wagon, and the procession moved with slow and solemn tread towards the dread instrument of death, the while the accompanying band played the "Dead March." On reaching the gallows, Kuhne alighted from the wagon and moved up the steps to the platform with a remarkably firm step. His spiritual advisors, Rev. Messrs. Kerfoot and A.A. Reese, accompanied him. He was dressed in fatigue uniform, with a small black shawl thrown over his shoulders. On reaching the scaffold an address was made by Mr. Reese, and prayer was offered by Mr. Kerfoot. The rope was adjusted on the neck of Kuhne by the acting provost marshal, who read the findings of the court-martial and the death warrant. When Col. Morris inquired if he had anything to say before his death, the doomed man replied that he had not. In another instant the trip fell with a dull, heavy sound, and Joseph Kuhne was suspended in mid-air ...the drop was only about eighteen inches but for a few moments no motion was observable. After which his contortions were horrible for a minute, after which he hung still and lifeless...."[44]

A private in the Fifth New York who witnessed the affair, stated that "...it was necessary, for the sake of military discipline, and as an example to others, that he should die." Private Kuhne was buried at the request of friends in Mount Carmel Cemetery in Baltimore.[45]

Andrew Laypole, *alias* Isadore Leopard
Captain, Confederate Army
Captured as a spy, bushwhacker and guerrilla.
Executed on May 23, 1864

In April of 1863, Captain A. Laypole, an alleged guerrilla, captured in Winchester, Virginia, was conveyed to Fort McHenry on May 4. In January 1864, a military commission found him guilty and sentenced him to be shot on May 23. *The Sun* recorded Laypole's fate:

"To be shot as a Guerrilla. — .....Shortly after five o'clock in the morning [the 23 year old] Leopard was placed in a cart and seated upon his coffin, and was conveyed to the scaffold, guarded by the Seventh Regiment Ohio Militia. The muffled drums, the slow and measured tread of the soldiers, imparted to the scene a feeling anything but pleasant to the spectator. On passing the other prison rooms [in the Sally Port prison] he waved his hand to his fellow prisoners, and to one of them who had a parole of the grounds he bade good-bye, and asked him to tell his friends that he died true to his country. Shortly after reaching the scaffold, around which was formed, in hollow square, a detachment of troops under Colonel Miller, of the One Hundred and Forty-Fourth Ohio Regiment .... [Leopard] made a short address to those around him, stating that he appeared as a felon, but there was one who knew he was not of that character. He said he freely forgave all having to do with his death ..... He then offered an extempore prayer to the Most High, on the conclusion of which the rope was placed around his neck, and everything being in readiness, the word was given and he was suspended in the air. He struggled but slightly, and is supposed to have died in about five minutes."[46]

It was noted that Laypole was "a desperate man, a Guerrilla chief, and a Spy and a Murderer of the blackest dye. To be hanged by the neck until dead..." He was buried in Elmwood Cemetery, Sheperdstown, West Virginia, his birthplace.[47]

George M. McDonald, alias M.M. Dunning
Private, Third Maryland Cavalry, USA
Arrested for desertion and murder.
Executed on September 21, 1864

In April 1864, McDonald, thirty-eight years old, was transferred from the military prison in Baltimore to Fort McHenry. In August he was tried for desertion and shooting the arresting officer, a crime for which he was to be executed on September 21. The following day *The Sun* reported:

"General Morris, commandant of the Fort, had charge of the execution, and a few moments after 9 o'clock the prisoner was marched from his cell in the Fort to the outside yard of the outer Fort, near where the gallows stand. The [1,200] soldiers were drawn up in a hollow square around the prisoner, and a squad of twelve men detailed to shoot the prisoner (who knelt on his knees beside his coffin and grave). The chaplain of the Fort rendered spiritual aid to the condemned. He informed General Morris that he had nothing to say but that his sentence was just, and he died a penitent man, death having no terror for him. The orders were given to prepare to fire. One line of soldiers retired on each side so as to give the squad the "clear fire," as the soldiers term it. The chaplain and the officers in charge of the prisoner bade him good-bye, and when left alone he stood stoical, merely giving the sign that he was ready. At twenty minutes before ten o'clock the order was given to fire, and almost simultaneous with the report of the rifles, the unfortunate prisoner dropped to the ground a lifeless corpse, and thus the stern and awful majesty of military law and discipline was satisfied. The remains of McDonald were interred in the soldier's grave at Fort McHenry."[48]

GARRISON LIFE

*D*uring the war the commander of Fort McHenry was Colonel William Walton Morris (1801-1865), Second U.S. Artillery. In 1820, he graduated last in his class of thirty at the U.S. Military Academy at West Point. A veteran of the Seminole and

Mexican Wars, he later served at various posts including Fort Taylor, Florida, 1850; Forts Hamilton and Wood in New York, 1850-1856; Fort Leavenworth, Kansas, 1857-1858; and Fort Ridgely, Minnesota, 1859-1861 before his appointment on May 1, 1861 as commander of Fort McHenry.

His possessed in his conduct as commander, "firmness, fortitude and faithfulness" to the service in which he was employed. Among his fellow officers of the old army, he was known as "Black Bill" for his swindling acuteness at the game of cards on more than one occasion.

Promotions for Morris while at Baltimore came quickly: May 14, 1861 — Lieutenant-Colonel, Fourth U.S. Artillery; November 1, 1861 — Colonel, Second U.S. Artillery; June 9, 1862 — Breveted Brigadier-General for meritorious service; December 10, 1865 — Breveted Major-General for faithful and meritorious services during the war. On December 11, at Fort McHenry, Morris died at the age of sixty-four.[49]

Throughout the war years, in addition to the regular garrison of the Second and Fourth U.S. Artillery, twenty-five state regiments encamped at Fort McHenry, the veritable fortress known to all who passed through as the birthplace of "The Star-Spangled Banner." The symbolic inspirational icon of the flag gave the fort and the Monumental City of Baltimore a unique place in American history and songsters of the period. For those who performed garrison duty at Fort McHenry certainly was a mixture of reverence for its historic past and the cultural and entertainment amusements found within a large seaport. One of the curiosities for the soldier who served here was a 13-inch British mortar shell that had fallen during the "perilous fight" in 1814, a reminder of the stories they had heard as young boys. Fifty years later, new history was being written by young boys and veterans of another war.

Religious services were held within the post chapel, built by the Methodists in 1840, that also served as the post library and schoolroom for officers' children. After services, one could visit the post cemetery that contained the remains of those who had once served here dating back to the 1790's. The cemetery was removed in 1895 and the remains relocated.

The two-storied post hospital (53' long and 27' wide) with piazzas, was built in 1840 with a capacity of sixty beds. Hospital tents were erected adjacent to the building for the accommodation of both Union and Confederate soldiers when the hospital rooms became insufficient for large numbers.

The seawall, which encompassed the 53 acres of the garrison, was a popular site for fishing, as well as nearby Busche's Ferry Bar, a popular resort for those who wished to escape the tedious routine of military life by bathing and the bountiful delicacies of soft crabs the Patapsco River had to offer.

From the ramparts of the star fort, one had a panoramic view of the Monumental City and its fortifications that loomed on the horizon upon the various natural promontories surrounding the city. For political prisoners, who shared the same view, "the stars and stripes" that flew from these posts reminded them of the "once proud emblem of American liberty." It was this fact that returned the soldier's various excursions to the realities of his position — that of guarding the prisoners who were constantly being sent and transferred from Fort McHenry.

The following two garrison accounts were written during the summer of 1864. Both provide a detailed and illustrative survey of life at Fort McHenry. The first was written by a Private Robert R. Moore, Co. D, Third Massachusetts Volunteers, while on duty from July 17 to August 17, 1864. They were relieved by the 192nd Pennsylvania Regiment.

Fort McHenry
Baltimore, Md
July 17, 1864

"Dear Mother:

I received your welcome letter day before yesterday, and was exceedingly glad to hear from you. I don't know whether this letter will interest you or not but I hope it will. I have drawn a picture of the fort the best I could for you know[ing] I am no kind of drawer. Now I suppose you have been under the impression that we have been quartered in the Fort but such is not the case as you will see by my drawing we are inside the fortifications but not inside the fort. This is what is called a birds-eye view or in other words you are supposed to be looking down from above.

Now you will see that this fort was never built to fire [upon] the city, its sole strength is pointing out in the bay [Patapsco River] and it can do considerable damage in that direction. Its largest guns and mortars are [now] turned on the city [of Baltimore]. Since this war, as you will remember Gen'l [John] Dix at one time threatened to shell the city [in 1861] and he turned his large guns on that side of the fort for that purpose. When this fort was built it was never expected that this country would be at war with itself.

Now the water battery is a good deal lower than the fort. If the enemy should take the lower or water battery they would have to scale the wall about 25 feet high to get to the fort. The upper tiers of guns in forts are always considered the best but they would have to do some tall fighting before they could take it too. The water battery has 41 guns in it, but in case the enemy should take it, the guns would not do them any good as they cannot be turned on the fort.

The round ring in the center of the fort is the reservoir that supplies the grounds with water. It is pumped full twice a day by the prisoners. The buildings on each side of the sally port are prisons. The one on the left [north wing] is the one that the ex-mayor of Washington [D.C., Walter Lennox] is confined in. He has already served two years [for] he is a political prisoner.

Stockades is wooden staves on posts set in the ground and are fixed so that infantry can fire through them in case a force is landed and the guns become useless. No. 16 is what is called the provost prison. Now this is the worst place to guard in the whole fort and there is a great deal of growling when the boys have to guard it. The exterior guards are guards that guard the [main] gate and the walls around the fortification. The interior guard [guards] the fort and nothing else.

Mother you will see by this drawing where my bunk is. It is No. 19 where the mark is in the corner. Every building in the fort is represented here. I cannot go into all the explanations or details but if you will only preserve this til I come home I will explain all. Mother I am ashamed of this letter and I hate to send it but I have got the drawing of the fort (and it is a good one too) and I don't like to tear it up. My pen is a miserable one as you will see by the writing. I have been all over the barracks to get a good one but cannot so I hope that you will excuse me and remember the inconveniences I am in. I am well and doing first rate. Tell Anna I will answer her letter tomorrow or next day. I am on guard at the prison tomorrow as you [will] know where I am. Write soon. One month from today our time is up.

From your Affec't Son, Robt. R. Moore[50]

On July 23, 1864, the Twentieth Pennsylvania Regiment, one-hundred day volunteers arrived in Baltimore at the Calvert Street Station of the Northern Central Railroad. From there the regiment marched a short distance and stacked their arms at Calvert and Fayette Streets. Having refreshed themselves the regiment proceeded northeast five miles to Camp Mankin and performed routine duties of camp life. On August 1

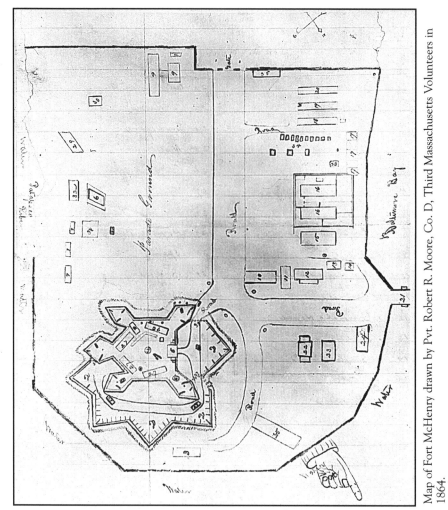

they struck camp and set off for the two hour march to Fort McHenry. While passing through Baltimore they passed the Battle Monument playing "The Star-Spangled Banner." Private John C. Meyer recorded and later published his regiment's sojourn in Baltimore, a city, Meyer noted that "was dying for want of rebels to seize the city, and are praying for them to come."

Meyer's comment reflected the Rebel offensive earlier in the Shenandoah Valley, crossing into Western Maryland under General Jubal Early which resulted in the Battle of the Monocacy on July 9. The following are excerpts from his journal.[51]

116

Statistics of Fort McHenry

#		#	
1	The Fort	22	Colonel French's House
2	Water Battery	23	Colonel Harris's Quarters
3	Armory	24	Wood Yard
4	Magazine	25	Miscellaneous Barracks
5	Sally Port	26	Old Generals Office in Fort
6	Bomb Proof Magazine	27	Palisades
7	Sutler	28	Hot Shot Furnaces
8	Carpenter Shop	29	Hospital Tent
9	Hospital	30	Spring
10	Quartermaster Dept.	31	Scaffold
11	Church	32	Store Houses
12	General's House	33	Tent
13	Bakery	34	Tents (Soldiers)
14	General's Stable	35	Guard House
15	Stable	36	Reservoir
16	Prisoners	37	Stockades
17	Cook House	38	Graveyard
18	Officers Barracks		
19	Company Barracks		
20	Company Barracks		
21	Pier where troops land		

O   Mortars
=   Ten inch Columbiads
O   Flagstaff
-   Guns
[ ] No. 19, my bunk

indicates the place (not far from the fort or position of the prison ship on which Francis Scott Key was confined when he composed "The Star-Spangled Banner."

Key to the map drawn by Private Moore.

Monday, August 1, 1864

"Reached the Fort at 12 [noon] pretty well fatigued. Found the 7th Ohio National Guard of Cincinnati in possession of the Fort, who soon vacated quarters, formed in line on the parade ground, and in a few moments they filed past our extensive line and went their way rejoicing for Ohio. Our guards were immediately detailed and posted. We were placed in very comfortable quarters, in tents and frame houses on the water side of the fort, fronting the city. There are some five hundred rebels confined here, among them are a few political prisoners ....."

Tuesday, August 2, 1864

"The regular routine of garrison duty occupied the attention of the officers and men all day .... Towards evening ....many of the boys rigged up fishing tackle for crab catching, and with very rude instruments, many haversacks were filled with this excellent shell fish .... First call for Reveille at early dawn; Reveille 15 minutes after first call; Fatigue; breakfast, 6 A.M.; Surgeon's call, 6:30; Guard Mounting, 7:30; Artillery drill, 9:00; Recall, 2 P.M.; Infantry drill, 3 P.M.; Recall, 4:30; Dress Parade, three quarters of an hour before sun-down; First call for Tattoo, 9:15; Taps, 9:30; Sunday morning inspection, 7:30 A.M.; Church call. 11 o'clock....."

Wednesday, August 3, 1864

"The day passed quietly. The heat was unabated in intensity until towards evening, when a cool river wind set in much to the relief of all ....The garrison band for the first time, passed along the regimental line at dress parade ...Religious services [were] held in the chapel this evening; regiment furnishing preacher, choir and congregation ...."

Thursday, August 4, 1864

"This day set apart by Congress for fasting and prayer, no military duty required, with the exception of guard mounting ....."

Friday, August 5, 1864

"Orders to-day changed the number of the regiment from the 20th to the 192nd Pennsylvania Volunteers, 8th Army Corps, under the command of Gen. Lew Wallace. A very large number of orders from General Headquarters were read at dress parade .... one prohibiting officers and men from loafing in the battlements of the fort, and forbidding soldiers appearing beyond their quarters in shirt-sleeves. Five rebel prisoners escaped from the hospital last night and are at large. There is something rotten in Denmark as to this escape, and the matter ought to be investigated ..."

Saturday, August 6, 1864

"Happened to be one of the guards on duty in the interior of the fort for 24 hours, on first relief ... [The fort's] largest rifled guns and villainous looking cohorns are pointed towards the city ....Each division contains a battery of from five to twenty heavy guns, some of them rifled pieces, with mortars and cohorns planted at intervals. Many of the heaviest, facing the city.

Happily the citizens of Baltimore returned to their allegiance and to their senses in time to save themselves from experiencing the dreadful consequences of their treason, although a large number of them, are still loyal ...

A well [in the center of the old fort] supplies water of good quality for the entire fort. The water is pumped into a tank, and the pump is worked with levers requiring from six to eight men. This pumping is done by deserters and bounty- jumpers, and soldiers sentenced by court-martial. They are obliged to pump from early dawn to taps, without ceasing, as a vast quantity of water is needed, which is the only freedom [prisoners are] allowed on the premises ..."

Sunday, August 7, 1864
"Late breakfast, owing to the absence of the bread rations. No fatigue duty to-day, and camp very quiet. The services in the chapel were attended by a very respectable congregation, and the choir was led by our popular surgeon, Dr. Kirk..."

Monday, August 8, 1864
"A very hot day and the tents too hot to live in them. Find relief along the shore line where some little current of fresh air can be found .... At 6 o'clock P.M., the whole regiment was marched into the ramparts of the fort, and the space accommodated all when in position in the rear of the guns. After glancing at these monster shooting irons for some ten minutes, and wondering all the time as to the object of the movement, the whole body upon the command to "about face" retreated from the fort and then dismissed ...."

Tuesday, August 9, 1864
"The regiment was called up at 5 o'clock A.M. at first call for Reveille, and marched into the exterior of the fort, facing the batteries. A lieutenant stationed the men in squads, the number required for the handling of each gun, some forty pieces. Each gun required a sergeant or corporal and five men. They counted off 1, 2, 3, 4, Gunner — two on each side of the piece, and the gunner at the centre of the breach. The exercise was deeply interesting and delighted the men beyond measure .... two hours were devoted to drill ..."

Wednesday, August 10, 1864
"A funeral and a death in the fort to-day. Second funeral since our arrival here. The deceased soldier [Charles Dornbush]

belonged to the regular army, and died of disease contracted in the service .... The usual duties of the fort were alone performed. There was no further artillery practice ....It was unofficially stated this morning that the regiment would retire from Fort McHenry to a post westward. Johnson's Island, Ohio [a federal prisoner of war prison] was indicated as our probable destination. During the time of our stay here, the whole command was fully employed .... Spare hours in the evening were often passed in singing patriotic and other songs, and it would be an injustice not to place some of them on record, so that when the war is over, somebody can sing them ..."

Thursday, August 11, 1864
"Between 12 and 1 o'clock this morning, troops, were heard marching into the fort, and at daylight, there was to be seen an entire regiment in repose, stretched on the grounds, and without tents. It was [the Fifth Massachusetts Regiment], and came for the purpose of relieving the 192nd. Preparations were at once commenced for the march to some other point. Bade adieu to Fort McHenry at 12 o'clock and marched to the depot of the Northern Central Railroad ....."

At 4 o'clock the 192nd departed Baltimore. Along the rail route Meyers noted that the loyal people "cheered and waved their hats, and every token of loyalty was given that could be desired or expected."

———◆•◆••◆———

Artillery Park at Fort McHenry: Note dismounted gun barrels in the background. From a stereoview taken about 1866.

VI

THE DEFENSES OF BALTIMORE

For many, when mention is made of the defenses of Baltimore during the war, attention is immediately focused upon Fort McHenry, which rivals Fort Sumter in Charleston as one of the best known forts in America. There were however, a series of forts, camps, and redoubts constructed during the Civil War which collectively became known as the Defenses of Baltimore. By the end of 1864, forty-two known fortified sites encircled Baltimore, guarding vital rail lines and places of encampment as regiments passed through during the war or as regional military engagements prompted additional security measures. The following is an outline of those forts that enabled the federal government to secure and maintain a strong Union presence in the Monumental City of Baltimore.

1861

*O*n May 7, 1861, the New York *Herald Tribune* published what may have been the first military map of an American city fortified by the federal government during the war. The drawing, made available to the *Tribune* by Major Henry Brewerton, U.S. Army Corps of Engineers, clearly shows

> "The points in Baltimore which should be held by military forces, whether for purposes of attack or occupation ....A force holding these three points [Murray's Hill, Patterson Park, Federal Hill], in addition to Fort McHenry, has the total command of the city, and, if necessary, can destroy it in a short time. The [map] also exhibits the relative position of the different [rail] lines entering the city, with the line of Pratt Street, where, the Massachusetts soldiers were treacherously murdered by the Secessionists."[1]

A good engineer, it is remarkable how immune Major Brewerton was to the concept of classified information.

After the war, Morgan Dix published the memoirs of his father, Major General John Dix, who took command of the Department of Maryland on July 23, 1861. His memoirs stated the military situation in the summer of 1861:

> "Maryland was substantially the military base of the operations on the Potomac. The loss of Baltimore would have been the loss of Maryland; the loss of Maryland would have been the loss of the national capital, and perhaps, if not probably, the loss of the Union cause." To the commanding officer at Fort Monroe, Dix asserted, "Baltimore has always contained a mass of inflammable material, which ignites on the slightest provocation. A city so prone to burst out into flame, and thus become dangerous to its neighbors, should be controlled by the strong arm of the Government....."[2]

At Baltimore, only Federal Hill rivals Fort McHenry's role in the Civil War, because of its natural promontory and presence over the har-

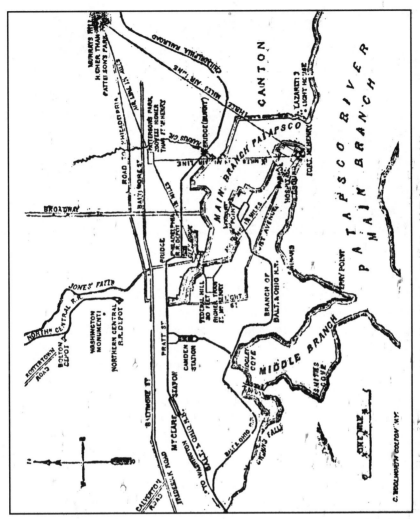

Military map of Baltimore published by the New York Herald Tribune in 1861.

bor even today. On May 13, it was the first city site to be occupied by federal forces when Brigadier General Benjamin Butler, fortified it with 1,000 troops for the purpose of enforcing "respect and obedience to the laws." As more federal troops arrived or passed through Baltimore, it became clear that the lines of communication for moving troops and supplies to Washington must be protected.

The answer to the dilemma that faced Dix, in the critical months of 1861, was to provide a visual military presence that would quiet any insurrection by Southern interests. In August, Dix surveyed the city's

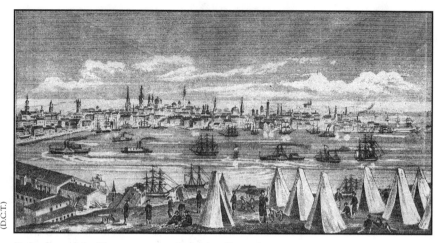

Early view of the Union camp on Federal Hill.

environs and listed those sites, viewed in the map published by the *Tribune*. The troops at these locations amounted to 4,633 men, many of whom were employed in building entrenchments. Detachments were sent to guard the bridges that carried the western rails of the Baltimore and Ohio Railroad into the city. The Thomas Viaduct at Relay and the Carrollton Viaduct in west Baltimore, as well as the Long Bridge and Sweitzer's Bridge, carried the roads to Annapolis and Washington over the Ferry Branch of the Patapsco River. This activity was further encouraged by a letter dated August 18 from General George B. McClellan to Brigadier-General Charles P. Stone, commanding the Division of the Potomac, warning of a "belief that the enemy intends crossing the Potomac in your vicinity and moving on Baltimore or Washington." The responsibility for constructing Baltimore's defenses through October 1864 fell upon Major Brewerton, a 60-year-old veteran of the U.S. Army Corps of Engineers who had replaced Robert E. Lee at Fort Carroll in 1852.[3]

Relay Junction — was the first site to be occupied outside of Fort McHenry. It was vital to the security of both Baltimore and Washington that the 612 foot stone-arched Thomas Viaduct (1835) remain intact over the Patapsco River and the main branch of the Baltimore and Ohio Railroad be protected. Three redoubts were built — Fort Dix, Camp Essex, and Camp Morgan. They were first manned by the Sixth Massachusetts and Eighth New York Infantry and the Boston Light Artillery. By the end of the war twenty-eight field guns were located at Relay and dozens of regiments had taken their turn guarding the railroad.[4]

Fort Federal Hill — The importance of Federal Hill (Fort No. 15) during the war was perhaps greater than Fort McHenry. This was due to its prominent location 89 feet above the harbor which gave it both a strategic and psychological value in maintaining military discipline at the doorstop of Baltimore's civil unrest. Its ordnance commanded the city's business district and surrounding harbor with sight lines to all fortifications.

On July 27, 1861, Colonel Abram Duryea's flamboyantly dressed Fifth New York "Duryea's Zouaves" occupied the hill along with a detachment of the Eighth New York Infantry. Major General John A. Dix, who commanded Baltimore's defenses, informed the War Department that "the hostile feeling which exists in the city and which does not even seek to disguise itself, indicates the absolute necessity of occupying and fortifying a commanding position nearer [to Baltimore] than Fort McHenry." A member of the Fifth New York commented on the works upon this prominent natural landmark:

"The regiment from its first arrival was engaged in the work of throwing up fortifications on Federal Hill, and it was some months before the soldier had any rest from the, to many of them, unaccustomed task of handling pick and shovel and spade from morning till night in digging the trenches, throwing up the ramparts, grading the glacis, forming the sally ports, the counter-scarps, the bastions of that large and well constructed fort, and mounting the [60] heavy guns on its barbettes and in its bastions.....When standing on the parapet the visitor can have but one opinion as to its commanding position; and in the event of an attack, it could resist any force brought against it ....while the columbiads and other siege guns, stationed at regular distances in the bastions and along the curtain, were admirably planted for dealing out death and destruction."[5]

By March 30, 1862, when the Zouaves departed having been relieved by the Third New York Regiment, the fort was completed.

The initial armament of the hill in September 1861 gave the federal government a formidable fortress; six 8-inch Columbiads, twenty-two 32-pounders, two light Howitzers, two 12-pounder Mountain howitzers, five 10-inch mortars, and five 24-pounder Sea Coast Howitzers — a total of forty-two guns, complete with three magazines containing 600 barrels of powder, together capable of reducing the southern waterfront of Baltimore to rubble.[6]

(D.C.T.)

Federal Hill or Fort No. 15 was more important than Fort McHenry during the war. Its cannon commanded the city's business district and surrounding harbor as shown by these photographs taken in 1870. (Top) looking northeast toward Fort McHenry. (Bottom) View of inner harbor with the Shot Tower in the background.

Murray Hill — also known as Potter's Race Course, was situated on the Canton Company's property about half a mile east of Patterson Park, upon a 132 foot high promontory. Its four-sided bastion earthen ramparts gave the hill a high profile easily distinguishable from all quarters of the city. The artillery proposed for the work consisted of four 8-inch Columbiads, six 42-pounder guns, eight 32-pounder guns, seven 24-pounder guns, and eight 8-inch Sea Coast Howitzers.[7]

McKim's Mansion — described by Dix as an "excellent and ample ground for battalion drill." The estate and home of merchant John S. McKim, built in 1787, was occupied in August 1861, by the Sixth Michigan Regiment. The following year it served as a hospital.[8]

(D.C.T.)

Unidentified member of the 7th New York Infantry. His regiment served in Fort Federal Hill.

Steuart's Mansion — was situated on the estate of General George Hume Steuart, bounded by West Fayette, Fulton Avenue, West Baltimore, and Smallwood Streets. Steuart resigned a commission to command in the Regular Army to become a lieutenant colonel in the First Maryland Infantry, C.S.A. His property and home were seized in 1861, by the Seventeenth Massachusetts Infantry who named their camp Mount Clare, after the nearby Baltimore and Ohio's Rail Depot and yards. In 1861, the Fourth Pennsylvania and the Second Maryland guarded this vital property and adjacent rail lines.[9]

Camp Carroll — in southwest Baltimore across from the Mount Clare Mansion, became a training depot for Maryland cavalry, infantry and light artillery regiments during the first two years of the war. In 1864 the Eleventh Maryland Infantry and First Maryland Cavalry were stationed there. Steuart's Mansion and Camp Carroll helped secure the Baltimore and Ohio Railroad and its Mount Clare Shops. In 1864 it became temporarily known as Camp Chesebrough after Assistant Adjutant W.G. Chesebrough.[10]

Battery, Steuart's Place: Envelope art depicting Federal camp on the estate of General George H. Steuart, C.S.A.

Patterson Park — was situated on land donated by William Patterson as a public park in 1827. This natural prominence rose 124 feet above high tide and overlooked the maritime community of Fells Point, one mile to the south. It was here, in 1814, that Baltimoreans rallied to defend the city. Remnants of the 1814 earthworks were still visible. The Seventh and Tenth Maine Regiments encamped here in 1861. During the war it served as a camp and a U.S. Army General Hospital.[11]

By the autumn of 1861, several other fortifications began to complete the encirclement of Baltimore. Municipal parks and private estates provided suitable sites for camps, recruitment rendezvous and defensive redoubts.

1862-1863

*T*hroughout 1862, and continuing through the war, the Baltimore newspapers, especially the Baltimore *American*, gave daily columns on troop movements as they bivouacked or moved through the city to the various theaters of war. As the war continued, these earlier sites were occupied by numerous state regiments who renamed them after the regiment's commander or well known state and military officials. Baltimore witnessed a military buildup to rival that of the nation's most fortified city, Washington, D.C., with its ninety-eight fortified positions.

To the north — Camp Melvale at Cold Spring Lane and Jones Falls was garrisoned by Colonel Ellsworth's Zouaves, Company A, Eighty-Seventh Pennsylvania Regiment. Along Charles Street, the expansive grounds of the Maryland Agricultural Society were taken for Camp Bradford, named after Maryland Governor Augustus Bradford, but referred to by the soldiers as Camp Cattleground. In 1862, it became a rendezvous for drafted men.[12]

Camp Belger — adjacent to Druid Hill Park (Fort No. 5), was occupied by the 114th and 150th New York Infantry, and named after Colonel James Belger, Quartermaster of the Middle Department. During the war, no less than fifteen regiments encamped here. In 1863, it became known as Camp Birney, after Major General William Birney, son of a Kentucky abolitionist, when he organized the Seventh U.S. Colored Troops here, followed by the Fourth and Thirty-Ninth U.S. Colored Troops in 1864.[13]

To the east — Patterson Park became Camp Washburn (Fort No. 12), briefly garrisoned in August 1861 by the Third Maryland, then by the Tenth Maine, who were relieved by the Seventh Maine. In 1862, Murray's Hill (Highlandtown today) became Fort Marshall or Fort No. 14. With 60 guns, it guarded the approach of the Philadelphia, Wilmington and Baltimore Railroad to the city.[14]

To the west — Camp Andrew (Fort No. 1 1/2), formerly Steuart's Mansion, was occupied by the Seventh Maine, who named it for the

(D.C.T.)

Fort Marshall or Fort No. 14: With 60 guns it guarded the P.W.&B. Railroad on the north side of the city.

131

Governor of Maine, John A. Andrews. Later it was referred to as Camp Wool (1862), Steuart's Grove, Camp Creager, Camp Reynolds, and finally Camp Simpson, for Major M. Simpson, Commissary for the Middle Department. In 1864, it became Jarvis General Hospital.[15]

To the south — lay Fort McHenry with its 72 guns and mortars, howitzers and columbiads, the largest and most heavily fortified garrison. Outside its gates was Camp Cadwalader, a rail and shipping depot, where troops, armament and supplies were waiting deployment from Locust Point. In July 1864, federal forces mobilized here prior to General Lew Wallace's advance to the Monocacy River. Four miles below, guarding the shipping channel was Fort Carroll, still under construction, but capable of mounting several batteries.

In September 17, 1862, as federal forces engaged the Army of Northern Virginia at Antietam, additional works were established while other former defenses were used for a succession of military installations, most notably as U.S. Army hospitals.

Other sites, continued to be occupied and renamed in a succession of troop maneuvering, especially in June of 1863, as the Gettysburg campaign began moving northward across Maryland. The Baltimore City Council appropriated $100,000 for the city's defense. On June 20, Major General Robert Schenck, commander of the Middle Department, Eighth Army Corps, informed Mayor Chapman, that "I am prepared, among other preparations for the defense of Baltimore against a possible attack of the Rebels, to construct some lines of fortifications at points commanding approaches to the city...." Thousands of citizens, black and white, were pressed into service day and night building barricades and earthen redoubts under the command of Lieutenant Meigs , U.S. Army Corps of Engineers.[16]

On June 29, communications revealed large bodies of Confederate cavalry were operating west and north of the city, cutting wires, rails being torn up, and bridges being burned, leading to rumors the Rebels were advancing. Martial law was declared as barricades were constructed closing the streets to vehicle traffic. Major General Schenck issued orders that "no one will be permitted to pass the barricades or into or out of the city between the hours of 10 p.m. and 4 a.m., without giving the proper countersign to the guard in charge." The defeat of the Rebel army at Gettysburg, and its retreat across the Potomac, left Baltimore once more safe in the hands of the occupying federal forces. On December 31 the Richmond *Examiner* observed, "Today closes the gloomiest year of our struggle."[17]

1864

*I*n the summer of 1864, Baltimore experienced a flurry of activity, similar to that of a year before, when the city was threatened by Lee's advancing army towards Gettysburg. Now, the South's third and final invasion of Maryland, led by General Jubal Early, advanced along the Monocacy, and brought renewed fears in the streets of Baltimore and Washington. On July 11, the City Defense Committee, consisting of the Mayor, the presidents of the two branches of the city council and two members were charged with the disbursement of a $100,000 defense appropriation. By August, twelve additional earthen redoubts were constructed in numeric sequence. Existing sites were reinforced to meet the Rebel invasion. Lieutenant John R. Meigs, U.S. Army Corps of Engineers (son of the Quartermaster General of the Army, Montgomery C. Meigs) was assigned the task of constructing the defenses in addition to street entrenchments and barricades.

Fort	Location	Armament
Fort No. 1	West Baltimore and Smallwood Sts.	10 field guns
Battery A	NE Cor. of Monroe and Ramsey Sts.	5 field guns
Fort No. 1/2	West Baltimore and Small Sts.	None
Fort No. 2	Franklin and Kirby's Lane	None
Fort No. 3	Franklin Street and Kirby's Lane	4 field guns
Fort No. 4	Townsend Street and Kirby's Lane	2 field guns
Fort No. 4 1/2	Gilmor and Baker Sts.	3 field guns
Fort No. 5	Druid Hill Park (Madison Avenue)	3 field guns
Fort No. 6	Druid Hill Park (Madison Avenue)	5 field guns
Fort No. 7	North Avenue and Madison Avenue	6 field guns
Fort No. 8	Valley and John Street	3 field guns
Fort No. 9	Harford and North Avenue	2 field guns
Fort No. 9 1/2	Caroline Street (Fells Point)	None
Fort No. 10	Caroline Street (Fells Point)	1 field gun
Fort No. 11	Chester and Elderry Streets	7 field guns
Fort No. 12	Fort Patterson Park	5 field guns
Fort No. 13	Fort Worthington (Kenwood and Preston Streets)	9 field guns[18]

General Morris had overall command of all the defenses. He divided this responsibility into two sectors. General John R. Kenly took charge of the fortifications west of the Jones Falls and General Henry Lockwood took those to the east of the Falls. Some of the redoubts were without ordnance and poorly garrisoned. Others bristled with guns from the

Junior Artillery and Eagle Artillery — both six month batteries more political than military in nature. To assist in garrisoning the under-manned fortifications, a Citizen Guards was organized and a "colored militia" put under General Lew Wallace's son. The Baltimore City police were augmented with citizens who wore special badges of identification. The Baltimore and Ohio Railroad moved all their available engines and cars to Locust Point for safekeeping. North of the city three federal gun-boats, the U.S.S. *Carituck*, U.S.S. *Teaser*, and the U.S.S. *Fuschia*, were stationed to guard the rail bridges over the Bush, Gunpowder and Susquehanna Rivers.[19]

The immense precautions undertaken by federal authorities to pro-tect Baltimore were never tested as the last Confederate offenses failed to reach the city. On July 15, *The Sun* stated, "The excitement in this city attending the invasion of this State by the Rebels has almost completely abated."[20]

VII

WAR MACHINE FOR THE UNION

The story of Baltimore's citizens attacking Pennsylvania and Massachusetts volunteers on the 19th of April, 1861, has been told in Chapter Two. From that day until the end of the war many in the North viewed the city purely as a rebel stronghold. This popular misconception has carried forth, for the most part unchallenged, to the present day. On April 21, 1861, a small group of shopkeepers from Fells Point went to a photography studio on South Broadway and had their picture taken with a United States flag. This quiet act of patriotism may have gone unnoticed in 1861, but in retrospect it represented the direction that Maryland as a state, and Baltimore as a city, would take in the future.[1]

From the colonial period until well after the War of 1812 Baltimore's social, economic and political activities were controlled by a slave-owning upper-class. In the middle of the city's social order was a small but steadily increasing merchant class. At the bottom were slaves, free blacks, and the largest segment of the population, poor whites. Evident after 1850 was an immigration from two vastly different origins that would put the same stress on Baltimore's social order that the western migration was putting on the balance of power in the United States Congress.

From Europe came the Germans, outnumbering the Irish two to one. The Germans were fleeing the failed Revolution of 1848. Most were educated and brought with them a marketable skill or trade. They were not interested in slavery and appreciated the freedom America had to offer. During the secession winter of 1860-61, the German language paper *Der Wecke* boldly stated "Within the Union happy, outside the Union unhappy." Embedded within the German community of Baltimore was a smaller number of German Jews. Aside from their religious differences, these immigrants shared the same language, schools, and newspapers as part of the overall German community. Most of these families would support the Union and prosper during the war. Other families like the Cohen's would be fractured over the question of states rights.[2]

The Irish fled famine and servitude to absentee landlords. They were for the most part illiterate and unskilled. The antipathy of the slave-owning upper-class, they would give little support for a secession movement. Suited only for hard labor they immediately began to displace blacks in the work force. Prior to 1850 blacks and hired slaves performed most of the tasks at the lower end of the labor market. Irish immigrants had no reservation about performing these tasks. At the same time poor whites had to compete with both the blacks and the Irish for jobs that had once been considered safely theirs. This triangle of competition for jobs disrupted the status quo by making slavery less profitable and free blacks an economic issue. New political power was also given to the ward bosses as the number of eligible voters increased.[3]

A less demonstrative group of immigrants which contributed to a shift in power over time was that of individuals from Northern states who saw a chance for advancement in the thriving port city of Baltimore. By 1860 many were wealthy industrialists such as Horace Abbott of

Massachusetts who in 1850 built the largest rolling mill in the United States at the Canton Iron Works and Enoch Pratt who made a fortune as a commissioned agent. When the war came, these men would align themselves with such figures as Johns Hopkins to support the Union from the very top of Baltimore's social order.[4]

As noted earlier, Baltimore, by 1861, was one of the largest industrial cities in the country. Its assets would have been a welcome addition to either government's war effort. Once Butler planted his cannon on Federal Hill these assets were irrevocably in the hands of the federal government. The first to be used were the railroads. The Philadelphia, Wilmington, and Baltimore ran due north of the city, connecting it to New York and Boston. The Northern Central ran in a northwesterly direction to Harrisburg, the capital of Pennsylvania and training ground for Union volunteers. On the south side of the city, the Baltimore and Ohio had a vast complex of stations, railyards, and workshops. At the Mount Clare shops locomotives, rolling stock, and bridge components were both manufactured and repaired. By 1863, 525 cars had been built and hundreds more would be completed before the end of hostilities. During the war Confederate forces repeatedly struck the main line of the railroad between Baltimore and Wheeling, West Virginia. After each attack trains would travel west from Mount Clare with new rails, bridges, and other stationary equipment. Eastbound trains would return with bent rails, damaged locomotives and the debris from stations and bridges. Tons of steel were recycled to the Mount Clare furnaces to make new rails. The enormous capacity of the Mount Clare shops enabled the B&O to repair the damage almost as fast as the rebels could inflict it. President Garrett worked very well with Secretary of War Stanton and President Lincoln to supply the needs of the federal government. He utilized his extensive system of telegraph offices and moving trains to gather information on enemy troops movements that Washington would have been ignorant of otherwise.[5]

A fourth railroad, the Western Maryland, ran from Westminister to the Relay House on the Northern Central. From there it ran into the city by a cooperative agreement on the Northern Central line. During the Gettysburg Campaign the Western Maryland moved tons of supplies and thousands of troops from Baltimore to the Army of the Potomac. After the battle of Gettysburg it brought back train loads of wounded and prisoners of war in the thousands.

The second element of transportation that cannot be overlooked was the shipping industry. Docks, shipyards, and the availability of hundreds of vessels, both steam powered and sail, gave a welcome boost to a Union

The Baltimore and Ohio Railroad carried thousands of soldiers and tons of supplies for the Union army during the war, making it a prime target for Confederate raiders. Damage was quickly repaired due to the efficiency of the Mount Clare shops.

(Leslie's Illustrated)

navy ill prepared for war. Locust Point became a major Union supply base of operations where military goods could be brought into the city by rail and loaded aboard ships for operations anywhere along the Atlantic coast. Shipyards and drydocks ringing the harbor could repair battle damage and construct new vessels.

The Locust Point docks witnessed throughout the war the arrival and departure of New York transports filled with government stores to the wharves, and thence to rail-cars for transportation to Washington. This venue of rail transportation, rather than by water up the Potomac River, was the result of the Confederate capture of the Norfolk Navy Yard and blockade of the river in 1861.

(D.C.T.)

Pier 9 Locust Point: Locust Point provided the main interchange point between ocean and rail traffic in the East during the war. This photograph taken ca. 1870 shows the same type of activity between rail, barge, and ocean going vessel.

At Locust Point, the Baltimore and Ohio Railroad ran day and night to convey, with the help of a large work force of laborers and government clerks, the provisions needed by the federal forces. The railroad also maintained a coal depot to supply steamers.

In October 1861, in one day, an estimated sixty vessels unloaded their stores into 200 cars, equal to nearly 2,000 tons of freight to be conveyed by the Baltimore and Ohio Railroad to the Mount Clare yards where the trains and freight were sorted, distributed, and dispatched to their destination. Mount Clare Depot also contained extensive facilities for horses, mules and cattle. Their provisions of oats and hay were conveyed as well. Artillery, ordnance munitions and equipage were also funneled through the Point as well as the disembarkation of thousands of troops.[6]

At the shipyard of Thomas H. Booz and Brothers, on Harris Creek, Canton, an extensive government contract was awarded to build pontoon bridges for the use of the army. Composed of a number of boats, each thirty-one feet long, when placed side by side, at a distance of twenty feet, with timbers laid across, could enable a column of soldiers, ten abreast, to be safely carried across a river. Constructed with the addition of wheels, each section or boat, could be used as baggage wagons.[7]

In 1862 the firm of H. Abbott & Sons provided armor plates for the turret of the USS *Monitor*. Abbott's Mill Number Two contained five furnaces, a Nasmyth steam hammer, and a pair of ten foot rollers, the largest in the country at the time. In all Abbott had four mills capable of producing tons of plates, gas pipes, and boiler tubes — all essential for the construction of war ships. The U.S. Navy's overall war strategy was reminiscent of World War II. The hull of the USS *Shamrock* was laid at the New York Navy Yard in 1863. Machinery for the side-wheeler was manufactured by Poole and Hunt in Baltimore and shipped north for installation.[8]

Three warships were constructed in their entirety by Baltimore firms. On October 3, 1861, the shipyard of Abrahams & Ashcroft at Thames Street, Fells Point, launched the United States gun-boat *Pinola*, amidst the salute of artillery and immense a crowd of curious citizens. She was then taken to the nearby Reeder's works for her machinery, to be ready for service in six weeks. The USS *Monocacy* was launched on December 14,1864, by A. & W. Denmead and Son in Canton. This 225-foot double-ended iron side-wheeler steamer weighed 1,370 tons and cost $275,000 to build, the largest warship built in Baltimore during the war. The third warship, also built by Denmead, was the USS *Waxsaw*, a monitor, launched on May 4, 1865.[9]

Iron and steel produced in Baltimore was used to build and repair ships for the U.S. Navy.

The Monitor *Waxsaw*: Built in Canton by A. & W. Denmead and Son.

A more expedient means of acquiring ships was for the government to purchase or lease them. At the outbreak of hostilities Baltimore was home to a number of steamboat companies operating on the Chesapeake Bay and up and down the Atlantic coast. They were the Baltimore Steam Packet Line, which was known as the Old Bay Line, the Weems Line, Merchants and Miner Transport Company, Eastern Shore Steamboat Company, and others. Some of these companies had extensive fleets, others only one or two vessels. The Old Bay Line was taken over by the federal government and operated between Baltimore and Old Point Comfort. One of its boats, the *Louisiana*, made up part of General Burnside's expedition to North Carolina. The government brought the *Joseph White* from the Merchants and Miner Line and converted it to a gunboat — the *McClellan*. The entire fleet of the Weems Line was taken over by the government in 1862. The first Baltimore steamboat purchased was the *Hugh Jenkins* of the Eastern Shore Steamboat Company. She was sunk twice but refloated each time. Two other boats of the line, the *Balloon* and the *Cecil*, were used to patrol the bay waters.[10]

In 1861 the Navy planned to improve the blockade of Charleston Harbor by filling old ships with stone and sinking them in the channels leading into the harbor. Two ships for the "stone fleet," as it was called, were purchased in Baltimore, the USS *Patriot* and the USS *W.L. Bartlet*. In addition to the various ships acquired by the Navy, a number of sailors and Marines were recruited from the Baltimore area.[11]

The prewar industrial complex of Baltimore City was also converted to wartime production. This did not happen at first because of the anti-government sentiment attached to the city after the Pratt Street Riot. William Pierce wrote to General Dix in August of 1861:

"The Union sentiment of Baltimore, is to be found in the laboring and mechanical classes, who are almost unanimously in favor of the government. But these are the classes who are suffering and have suffered, so severely from the discrimination made by the government against Baltimore, and in favor of Philadelphia and the North, on the important matter of purchasing supplies of precious clothing, building ships, etc., for the army and the government. Baltimore is passed over and supplies obtained elsewhere at higher prices than those at which she is prepaid to furnish them."[12]

Realizing the untapped potential of Baltimore's factories, the federal government soon began to issue contracts for cotton, flour, iron, canvas sail cloth, and other products. One thousand boxes of shot, grape, and canister were shipped to Commodore John Rogers' fleet of gunboats at Cincinnati, Ohio. The cotton mills of Gambrills, Hooper, and Garys made tents for the army.[13]

On West Baltimore Street, the (James H.) Merrill Patent Fire Arm Company (1861-1866) produced in an arrangement with the Remington Company of New York, a total of 14,695 .54 caliber breech-loading percussion carbines for the U.S. Cavalry and the U.S. Navy. The company was briefly suspended by federal authorities in November 1861, but soon resumed operations.[14]

As a result of Baltimore's six decades of growth before the war, a considerable amount of capital existed in the banks and trading firms of the city. When the sale of government bonds dropped off in 1863 a federal banking law was amended to allow for the creation of national banks using government bonds as a basis for issuing bank notes. Johns Hopkins immediately secured a group of investors and chartered the First National Bank of Baltimore. Bond sales were rejuvenated and the banking venture was a complete success.[15]

One of the greatest resources released to the Union after the occupation of Baltimore in 1861 was manpower. Maryland enlistments in the Union army outnumbered those in the Confederate army three to one. This is not surprising given the shift in population and political attitudes during the 1850's. Without question those Maryland men who went South were true patriots to their cause. They risked everything in leaving their native state and running the blockade to fight in what many considered the second American Revolution. Their contribution can never be depreciated. However it is not far from the truth to say that an even larger number of men with the same dedication and resolve have all but been forgotten. They are the volunteers of 1861 and 1862 who enlisted for three years to preserve the Union. Throughout the course of the war all or part of sixteen infantry regiments, two cavalry regiments, and six batteries of artillery were recruited in Baltimore City.[16]

In 1861 William H. Purnell, Postmaster of Baltimore City, organized a combined arms force known as the Purnell Legion. Five companies of infantry came from the city. In 1862 Governor Bradford formed a committee of fifty Baltimore citizens led by John Pendleton Kennedy to aid in the enlistment of troops. The committee received the backing of Mayor Chapman and the City Council who appropriated $300,000 for bounties for state volunteers. When the decision was reversed by the lower branch of the council two days later, a mob threatened to hang several of the council members. It took one hundred policemen to protect John W. Wilson, one of the councilmen. Pressure from General Wool and the Union League caused nine members to resign. On September 5, the money was reinstated by a second vote which included new council members.[17]

On July 28, 1862, the Union League and the Union City Convention met with Governor Bradford to discuss ways to increase enlistments. It was diffi-cult to meet the continued gov-ernment levies when such a large portion of the population worked for the railroad, joined the Confederate army, or left the country until after the war was over. During the emergency call of 1863 all but one company of men from the Ninth and Tenth Maryland Volunteers came from Baltimore. In 1864 all of the Eleventh Maryland Regiment came from the city as well as two batteries of artillery.[18]

William H. Hunter: Chaplain of the Fourth United States Colored Troops. Enlisted in Baltimore on October 10, 1863.

Circular No. 1 dated October 26, 1863, called for the Bureau of Colored Troops to establish nineteen recruiting stations in the state of Maryland. Under the direction of Colonel William Birney and later Colonel S.W. Bowman, the Fourth Regiment United States Colored Troops was enlisted in the city. Later three companies of the Seventh U.S. Colored Troops and most of the Thirty-ninth U.S. Colored Troops were also recruited in Baltimore.[19]

In 1861 the first U.S. General Hospital was opened in Baltimore. Known as the National Hospital it took its name from the National Hotel which along with five other buildings formed a complex on either side of Camden Street across from the B&O Station. It was ideally situ-ated to receive wounded soldiers and Confederate prisoners of war arriv-ing by train. The hospital remained in operation throughout the war and had a capacity of 500 beds.[20]

The summer campaigns of 1862 resulted in a steady stream of wound-ed and sick soldiers being sent to Baltimore. Three more general hospi-tals were opened. The Wests Buildings General Hospital consisted of six

Interior view of a U.S. General Hospital.

former cotton warehouses located on Union Dock in southeast Baltimore. They were leased from Mr. William West, a resident of the city. Because of its location near water transportation, it was used as a distribution point for thousands of Rebel soldiers captured in Maryland and Virginia. The wounded were treated and their condition evaluated. Those able to travel were put aboard transports waiting at the wharf to take them to Fort Delaware, Point Lookout, or Fort Monroe. Union soldiers were also processed through this facility and sent on to hospitals in the North.[21]

The Newton University buildings on Lexington Street were converted into a 200 bed hospital. It was located near the 1814 Battle Monument — scene of many political events before and during the war. The property around the old John McKim Mansion was also appropriated for use as a hospital. The site was originally a fortified camp with earthworks and several two-storied wooden barracks. The barracks were converted to wards for U.S. Colored Troops. The mansion house was used as headquarters for their surgeons and their staffs. The complex became known as the McKim's Hospital. The estate of General George Hume Steuart, C.S.A. was appropriated as a campsite and later a hospital. Each new regiment that occupied the grounds changed the name of the camp, but the complex was always referred to as Steuart's Grove. It was located on high ground overlooking the city at the western end of Baltimore Street. The hospital was named Jarvis Hospital after Dr. Nathan S. Jarvis, Medical Director of the Department of Maryland.

(D.C.T.)

McKim's Hospital: U.S. Colored Troops were treated here.

Lt. H. A. Montgomery: Commanded the guard detail at Patterson Park Hospital.

During the first nine months of 1864, a total of 3,240 patients were treated of which 105 died.[22]

In 1863 the barracks of the Nineteenth Pennsylvania Infantry at Camp Patterson Park were converted to hospital wards with a 1,200 bed capacity. In 1864, 6,459 patients were treated with only 45 deaths. The last general hospital to open was named for Governor Thomas H. Hicks, Maryland's first wartime governor. It was located at the intersection of Pulaski Street and Lafayette Avenue in northwest Baltimore. The facility did not begin to receive patients until May of 1865 and was never fully utilized.[23]

Whether soldiers were passing through the city on their way to the front, assigned as occupation troops, or new recruits forming regiments of Maryland Volunteers, their needs, both physical and spiritual, were attended to by an array of national organizations and small local groups of concerned citizens. As early as May of 1861, the Baltimore Christian Association was organized. One month later the United States Sanitary Commission began its nationwide operation. The Association became the Baltimore Chapter of the U.S. Sanitary Commission. It was the Civil War version of the Red Cross and the USO all in one. Its counterpart, the United States Christian Commission, concentrated on the religious needs of the men in uniform. However, due to the overwhelming number of casualties after each campaign, they too supplied doctors, nurses, and medical supplies to both field hospitals and those in the city.

After the battle of Gettysburg the Baltimore Chapter of the Christian Commission leased four floors of the Apollo Hall for the storage and distribution of supplies and religious material. Fifteen people were employed full time as well as several volunteers to pack and ship standardized "cases" and special ordered items to hospitals and camps in Maryland, Virginia, and Pennsylvania as well as Baltimore City. Between

Church Home: Existing civilian hospitals were also utilized to care for military personnel. This 1870's photograph shows the Church Home Hospital with Wildy Monument in the foreground. The monument was dedicated on April 26, 1865, to Thomas Wildy, the founder of the Order of Odd Fellows in America.

November of 1862 and September of 1864, 1,070 "cases" had been distributed as well as thousands of bibles, hymn books, and other reading materials. During this same period 438 volunteers were sent into the field.[24]

Small organizations looked after the soldiers' needs in different parts of the city. The Ladies West End Union Relief Association worked at the Jarvis General Hospital to provide clothing, bandages, and food to the patients. Ladies of the Association of Newton University Hospital printed a flyer in which they described the condition of the patients and solicited items. "Under-clothes, shoes, slippers, and socks are very much needed." The Maryland State Bible Society was also active. Soldiers were

given small testaments with an information sheet glued inside the front cover. On this sheet the soldier was to write his name, company, regiment, and the name and address of someone to be notified "Should I die

Bible House, Baltimore,

March 27th 1864

From the Maryland State Bible Society

To James Robberts Soldier in

Comp'y M Reg. 1st Md bel Vol's.

Should I die on the battle field or in

Hospital, for the sake of humanity; acquaint

My Friends residing

at Nº 56 Washington St Balto

of the fact, and where my remains may be found.

[Pearl 32mo.]

AMERICAN BIBLE SOCIETY,
INSTITUTED IN THE YEAR MDCCCXVI.

NEW YORK:

1864.

THE FORMER TRANSLATIONS DILIGENTLY COMPARED AND REVISED.

AND WITH

THE ORIGINAL GREEK;

TRANSLATED OUT OF

LORD AND SAVIOUR JESUS CHRIST:

OF OUR

NEW TESTAMENT

THE

Bible of Pvt. James Roberts, Co. M, 1st Maryland Cavalry: The Maryland Bible Society gave soldiers Bibles with information sheets inside the front cover for notification of next of kin. Pvt. Roberts' friends resided at "No. 56 Washington St Balto."

on the battlefield or in hospital....." One agent for the society, Mr. Baker, alone distributed 13,500 testaments and 590 bibles at the Point Lookout Prison in Southern Maryland in 1864. By 1865 Baltimore City had truly become a war machine for the Union.[25]

William R. Clark: Killed on the 19th of April during the Pratt Street Riot.

APPENDIX

A

CASUALTIES,
PRATT STREET RIOT,
APRIL 19, 1861

The following is the official list of the killed and wounded of the Sixth Massachusetts Regiment during the Pratt Street Riot in Baltimore on April 19, 1861.

Source: *Historical Sketch of the Old Sixth Regiment of Massachusetts Volunteers*, by John W. Hanson, Chaplain (Lee and Shepard, Boston, Massachusetts, 1866).

4-Killed

Luther C. Ladd	Co. D	Charles A. Taylor	Co. D
Sumner H. Needham	Co. L	Addison O. Whitney	Co. D

36-Wounded

Serg. John E. Ames	Co. D	John W. Kimpton	Co. L
Daniel Brown	Co. L	Serg. W.H. Lamson	Co. D
Charles H. Chandler	Co. D	George W. Lovrein	Co. D
Edward Coburn	Co. D	Lt. Leaner F. Lynde	Co. L
George Colgan	Co. K	James S. Moody	Co. L
Horace W. Danforth	Co. L	Ira W. Moore	Co. D
Henry Dike	Co. L	William R. Patch	Co. D
Capt. John H. Dike	Co. L	Ephraim A. Perry	Co. L
Serg. Geo.G. Durrell	Co. I	Julian Putnam	Co. L
Stephen Flanders	Co. L	Andrew Robbins	Co. L
Henry Gardner	Co. K	Lt. James F. Rowe	Co. L
Alexander George	Co. D	Daniel C. Stevens	Co. D
Charles L. Gill	Co. L	Charles B. Stinson	Co. C
Victor G. Gingass	Co. I	Daniel B. Tyler	Co. D
Michael Green	Co. I	George T. Whitney	Co. K
William D. Gurley	Co. K	Wm. G. Withington	Co. D
Harry G. Jewell	Co. I	William H. Young	Co. L
James Keehan	Co. L		

The 26th and 27th Regiment Pennsylvania Volunteer Infantry, "The Washington Brigade."

John Greaves

Lineous Jennings

George Leisenring

Peter Rogers

Albert G. Rowland, 1st Lt.

List of the Citizens of Baltimore Killed

Source: *The Chronicles of Baltimore*, by Col. J. Thomas Scharf (Turnbull Brothers, Baltimore, Md., 1874)

11-Killed

James Carr

William R. Clark

Robert W. Davis

Sebastian Gill

Patrick Griffth

John McCann

Francis Malony

William Malony

Philip S. Miles

Michael Murphy

William Reed

APPENDIX
B

*M*ARYLAND! MY MARYLAND!

*O*n May 31, 1861, nearly forty days since the events that inspired it occurred on Pratt Street in Baltimore on April 19, *The South* published the poetic account. Later the editor, Thomas W. Hall, was arrested and imprisoned at Fort McHenry. It was written by a young Marylander, James Ryder Randall, a twenty-two-year-old teacher of English literature at Poydras College, Pointe Coupee, Louisiana. Having read about the riot in the Delta on April 23, he wrote these words, that became the battle hymn of Maryland Southerners. In 1939, the General Assembly of Maryland made it the official state song of Maryland.

(Tune: "Tannenbaum, O Tannenbaum")

The depot's heel is on thy shore,
Maryland!
His torch is at thy temple door,
Maryland!
Avenge the patriotic gore
That flecked the streets of Baltimore
And be the battle queen of yore,
Maryland! My Maryland!

Hark to an exiled son's appeal,
Maryland!
My mother State! to thee I kneel,
Maryland!
For life and death, for woe and weal,
Thy peerless chivalry reveal,
And gird they beauteous limbs with steel,
Maryland! My Maryland!

Thou wilt not cower in the dust,
Maryland!
Thy beaming sword shall never rust,
Maryland!
Remember Carroll's sacred trust,
Remember Howard's warlike thrust, -
And all thy slumberers with the just,
Maryland! My Maryland!

Come! 'tis the red dawn of the day,
Maryland!
Come with thy panoplied array,
Maryland!
With Ringgold's spirit for the fray,
With Watson's blood at Monterey,
With fearless Lowe and dashing May,
Maryland! My Maryland!

Come! for thy shield is bright and strong
Maryland!
Come! for thy dalliance does thee wrong,

Maryland!
Come to thine own heroic throng,
Stalking with Liberty along,
And chant thy dauntless slogan song,
Maryland! My Maryland!

Dear Mother! burst thy tyrant's chain,
Maryland!
Virginia should not call in vain,
Maryland!
She meets her sisters on the plain-
"Sic semper!" 'tis the proud refrain
That baffles minions back again,
Maryland! My Maryland!

I see the blush upon thy cheek,
Maryland!
For thou wast ever bravely meek,
Maryland!
But lo, there surges forth a shriek
From hill to hill, from creek to creek-
Potomac calls to Chesapeake,
Maryland! My Maryland!

Thou wilt not yield the Vandal tool,
Maryland!
Thou wilt not crook to his control,
Maryland!
Better the fire upon thee roll,
Better the blade, the shot, the bowl,
Than crucifixion of the soul,
Maryland! My Maryland!

I hear the distant thunder-hum,
Maryland!
The Old Line's bugle, fife, and drum,
Maryland!
She is not dead, nor deaf, nor dumb-
Huzza! she spurns the Northern scum!
She breathes! she burns! she'll come! she'll come!
Maryland! My Maryland!

APPENDIX
C

*L*INCOLN'S
SANITARY FAIR SPEECH,
APRIL 18, 1864

Delivered by President Abraham Lincoln at the Maryland Institute Hall
for the benefit of the U.S. Sanitary and Christian Commissions
Source: *The* [Baltimore] *Sun*, April 19, 1864.

Ladies and Gentlemen — Calling to mind that we are gathered in
Baltimore, we cannot fail to note that the world moves. Looking upon
these many people, assembled here, to serve, as they best may, the soldiers of the Union, it occurs at once that three years ago, the same soldiers could not as much as pass through Baltimore. The change from
then until now, is both great and gratifying. Blessings on the brave men

who have wrought the change, and the fair women who strive to reward them for it.

But Baltimore suggests more than could happen within Baltimore. The change within Baltimore is part only of a far wider change. When the war began, three years ago, neither party, nor any man, expected it would last till now. Each looked for the end, in some way, long ere to-day. Neither did any anticipate that domestic slavery would be much effected by the war. But here we are; the war has not ended, and slavery has been much effected — how much needs not now to be recounted. So true is it that men proposes, and God disposes.

But we can see the past, though we may not claim to have directed it; and seeing it, in this case, we feel more hopeful and confident for the future. The world has never had a good definition of the word liberty, and the American people, just now, are much in want of one. We all declare for liberty; but in using the same word we do not all mean the same thing. With some the word liberty may mean for each man to do as he pleases with himself, and the product of other men's labors. Here are two, not only different, but incompatible things, called by the same name — liberty. And it follows that each of the things is, by the respective parties, called by two different and incompatible names — liberty and tyranny.

The shepherd drives the wolf from the sheep's throat, for which the sheep, thanks the shepherd as a liberator, while the wolf denounces him for the same act as the destroyer of liberty, especially as the sheep was a black one. Plainly the sheep and the wolf are not agreed upon a definition of the word liberty; and precisely the same difference prevails to-day among us human creatures; even in the North, and all professing to love liberty. Hence we behold the processes by which thousands are daily passing from under the yoke of bondage, hailed by some as the advancer of liberty, and bewailed by others as the destruction of all liberty. Recently, as it seems, the people of Maryland have been doing something to define liberty; and thanks to them that, in what they have done, the wolf's dictionary has been repudiated.

It is not very becoming for one in my position to make speeches at great length; but there is another subject upon which I feel that I ought to say a word. A painful rumor, true I fear, has reached us of the massacre, by the rebel forces, at Fort Pillow, in the West end of Tennessee, on the Mississippi river, of some three hundred colored soldiers and white officers, who had just been overpowered by their assailants. There seems to be some anxiety in the public mind whether the government is doing its duty to the colored soldier, and to the service, at this point.

At the beginning of the war, and for some time, the use of colored troops was not contemplated; and how the change of purpose was wrought, I will not now take time to explain. Upon a clear conviction of duty I resolved to turn that element of strength to account; and I am responsible for it to the American people, to the Christian world, to history, and on my final account, to God. Having determined to use the Negro as a soldier, there is no way but to give him all the protection given to any other soldier.

The difficulty is not in stating the principle, but in practically applying it. It is a mistake to suppose the government is indifferent to this matter, or is not doing the best it can in regard to it. We do not to-day know that colored soldier, or white officer commanding colored soldiers, has been massacred by the rebels when made a prisoner. We fear it, believe it, I may say, but we do not know it. To take the life of one of their prisoners, on the assumption that they murder ours, when it is short of certainly that they murder ours, might be too serious, too cruel a mistake. We are having the Fort Pillow affair thoroughly investigated; and such investigations will probably show conclusively how the truth stands. If, after all that has been said, it shall turn out that there has been no massacre at Fort Pillow, it will be almost safe to say there has been none, and will be none elsewhere. If there has been the massacre of three hundred there, or even the tenth part of three hundred, it will be conclusively proved; and being so proved, the retribution shall as surely come. It will be a matter of grave consideration in what exact course to apply the retribution; but in the supposed case, it must come.

APPENDIX
D

*M*ILITARY ORGANIZATION OF BALTIMORE AND FORT McHENRY

*T*he organization of military divisions and geographic departments changed frequently during the war, especially the Middle Department, Eighth Army Corps, that makes it often difficult to understand the administrative logistics in Maryland. The following is intended only as a brief outline of the primary departments and their commanders that governed Baltimore during the war.

Sources:

The Union Army, 1861-1865: Organization and Operations, Volume 2, The Eastern Theatre, by Frank J. Welcher, (University of Illinois Press, 1989).

"U.S. Military Returns for Fort McHenry, 1861-1865," M-617, Roll 96, National Archives.

DEPARTMENT OF ANNAPOLIS

Established: April 27, 1861 to secure rail and telegraph communications between Annapolis, Washington and Baltimore with headquarters at Annapolis.

Geographic Area: All Maryland counties 20 miles on either side of the Baltimore and Annapolis Railroad from Annapolis to Washington including Baltimore.

Commanders	Dates	
Maj. Gen. Benjamin F. Butler	04/27/1861	05/15/1861
Maj. Gen. George Cadwalader	06/11/1861	06/23/1861
Maj. Gen. Nathaniel Banks	06/23/1861	07/21/1861

Changed to the:

DEPARTMENT OF MARYLAND

Established: July 21, 1861 with headquarters at Baltimore.

Geographic Area: Baltimore, Annapolis, Relay and Annapolis Junctions

Commander	Dates	
Maj. Gen. John Adams Dix	07/21/1861	07/23/1861

Merged into the:

DEPARTMENT OF PENNSYLVANIA

Established: April 25, 1861 with headquarters in Philadelphia.

Geographic Area: States of Pennsylvania, Delaware and Maryland not embraced in the Department of Annapolis.

Commanders	Dates	
Maj. Gen. Robert Patterson	04/29/1861	07/25/1861
Maj. Gen. John A. Dix	07/25/1861	08/24/1861

Merged into the Department of the Potomac

MIDDLE DEPARTMENT

Established: March 22, 1862 to administer and protect rail and communication lines of the Baltimore and Ohio Railroad, the Baltimore, Wilmington and Baltimore Railroad, and the Northern Central Railroad.

Geographic Area: New Jersey, Pennsylvania, Delaware and the Eastern Shores of Maryland and Virginia, and the Maryland counties of Cecil, Harford, Baltimore and Anne Arundel.

Commanders	Dates	
Maj. Gen. John Adams Dix	03/22/1862	06/09/1862
Maj. Gen. John E. Wool	06/09/1862	07/22/1862

BRIGADES / Middle Department — To provide better administration within the Middle Department the following brigades were provided.

Railroad Brigade — Organized in November 1861. On March 17, 1862, was commanded by Colonel Dixon S. Miles to protect the Baltimore and Ohio Railroad westward to Harpers Ferry where he established his headquarters. On July 22, 1862, it was redesignated Railroad Brigade, Middle Department, Eighth Army Corps.

Lockwood's Brigade — Organized on March 16, 1862, and commanded by Brigadier General Henry H. Lockwood to oversee operations on the Eastern Shore of Maryland and Virginia. See First Separate Brigade.

Armory's Brigade — Organized on March 27, 1862, and commanded by Thomas J.C. Armory and subsequently ordered to Hatteras, North Carolina, under General Burnside.

Cooper's Brigade — Organized in April 1862 and commanded by General James Cooper, a native of Frederick, Maryland, who commanded the troops stationed at Cockeysville, Havre de Grace, Mount Clare and McKim's Mansion in Baltimore. The brigade was disbanded on May 25, 1862. See Second Separate Brigade.

MIDDLE DEPARTMENT / EIGHTH ARMY CORPS

Established: On June 22, 1862, all troops from the Middle Department were redesignated Middle Department, Eighth Army Corps. The troops assigned served primarily in the defenses of Baltimore and various posts along the rail lines.

Geographic Area: On September 2, 1862, the limits of the department were extended to include all of Maryland. Discontinued August 1, 1865.

Commanders	Dates	
Maj. Gen. John E. Wool	07/22/1862	12/22/1862
Maj. Gen. Robert C. Schenck	12/22/1862	03/12/1863
Brig. Gen. William W. Morris	03/12/1863	03/20/1863
Maj. Gen. Robert C. Schenck	03/20/1863	08/10/1863
Brig. Gen. William W. Morris	08/10/1863	08/31/1863
Maj. Gen. Robert C. Schenck	08/31/1863	09/22/1863
Brig. Gen. William W. Morris	09/22/1863	09/28/1863
Brig. Gen. Erastus B. Tyler	09/28/1863	10/10/1863
Maj. Gen. Robert C. Schenck*	10/10/1863	12/05/1863
Brig. Gen. Henry H. Lockwood	12/05/1863	03/22/1864
Maj. Gen. Lew Wallace**	04/22/1864	02/01/1865
Maj. Gen. William W. Morris	02/01/1865	04/19/1865
Maj. Gen. Lew Wallace	04/19/1865	07/18/1865

* Schenck resigned on December 5, 1863, to take his seat in Congress.
** Edward O. Ord was assigned command of the Eighth Corps on July 11 during Jubal Early's Washington raid. Active command was returned to Wallace on July 28, 1864, when Ord was relieved.

SEPARATE BRIGADES / MIDDLE DEPARTMENT, EIGHTH ARMY CORPS

In 1863 three brigades were created from the Middle Department.

First Separate Brigade — On February 14, 1863, Lockwood's command was designated the First Separate Brigade and served in the Eastern Shore of Maryland and Virginia, with headquarters at Drummondtown, Virginia.

Commanders	Dates
Henry H. Lockwood *	02/14/1863 – 06/25/1863
	10/21/1863 – 12/18/1863
Erastus B. Tyler **	12/18/1863 – 11/17/1864
John R. Kenly	11/17/1864 – 12/13/1864
Erastus B. Tyler	12/13/1864 – 06/05/1865

* In June the brigade was ordered placed under the command of Joseph Hooker during the Gettysburg campaign, and on October 21 was reorganized.
** Troops were engaged at the Battle of Monocacy under Wallace's command.

Second Separate Brigade — (Defenses of Baltimore) On January 5, 1863, the defenses of Baltimore (known as "Dix's Command" in 1862) were organized into a separate brigade and on February 14, 1863, it was redesignated as the Second Separate Brigade to be commanded by Major General William W. Morris with headquarters at Fort McHenry. On July 29, 1863, it was re-created during the Gettysburg campaign and was assigned to Brigadier General Erastus B. Tyler. Included within the command were Forts McHenry, Marshall, Federal Hill and Fort Dix at Relay Junction.

Commanders	Dates
William W. Morris	01/05/1863 – 01/20/1864
Peter A. Porter	01/20/1864 – 05/10/1864
William W. Morris	05/10/1864 – 01/31/1865
Daniel McCauley	01/31/1865 – 04/19/1865
William W. Morris	04/19/1865 – 07/29/1865

Third Separate Brigade — From the Second Brigade was organized on February 14, 1863, under the command of Henry S. Briggs, whose command performed the duties of guarding various sites in Baltimore and the Baltimore and Ohio Railroad to Frederick, Maryland, and to Annapolis Junction.

On July 16, 1863, it was reorganized following the Gettysburg campaign, then discontinued on August 10, until October 21 when it was reorganized under the command of Erastus B. Tyler.

On December 18, 1863, it was merged with the First Separate Brigade until March 3, 1864, when it was reorganized to include the counties of Baltimore, Frederick, Carroll, and Harford, and the Maryland Eastern Shore.

Commanders	Dates
Henry S. Briggs	02/14/1863 – 06/25/1863
Samuel A. Graham	07/16/1863 – 08/10/1863
Erastus B. Tyler	10/21/1863 – 12/18/1863
Henry H. Lockwood	03/24/1864 – 05/20/1864
John R. Kenly *	05/16/1864 – 07/20/1864
Henry H. Lockwood	07/20/1864 – 07/31/1865

* Kenly was relieved on July 13 and assigned to a new brigade in Harpers Ferry. On March 12, Fort Delaware, a prisoner of war prison, was detached from the Middle Department to report directly to the War Department.

OFFICE OF THE PROVOST MARSHAL

Established: May 5, 1861, to oversee military occupation, investigate cases of disloyalty, treason, espionage, blockade running, etc. Discontinued: January 28, 1866.

Provost Marshal	Dates	
George R. Dodge (Civilian)	05/01/1861	06/24/1861
Col. John R. Kenly, 1st Maryland	06/24/1861	07/11/1861
Maj. William P. Jones, Conn. Vol.	07/11/1861	11/11/1862
Maj. Constable	11/11/1862	01/01/1863
Maj. William S. Fish	01/01/1863	01/15/1864
Maj. Z.H. Hayner	01/15/1864	03/24/1864
Lt. Col. John Wooley, 5th Ind. Cavalry	03/24/1864	01/28/1866

COMMANDERS OF FORT McHENRY

On May 1, 1861, Major William W. Morris (1801-1865), Fourth U.S. Artillery arrived from Fort Snelling, Minnesota, to take command of Fort McHenry remaining until his death on December 11, 1865. While in command, Morris served additional duties at times commanding the Eighth Army Corps. On May 14, 1861, he was promoted to Lieutenant Colonel, Second U.S. Artillery, and on November 1, promoted to Colonel. On June 9, 1862, he was promoted to Beveted Brigadier General, and on June 24 was placed in command of all the forts in Baltimore.

Commanders	Month	Year
Capt. Joseph A. Haskin, 1st U.S. Artillery	January	1861
Capt. John C. Robinson, 5th U.S. Infantry	February-April	1861
Major Wm. W. Morris, 4th U.S. Artillery	May-July	1861
Lt. Col. Wm. W. Morris, 4th U.S. Artillery	August-October	1861
Lt. Col. Wm. W. Morris, 2nd U.S. Artillery	November	1861–
	May	1862
Bvt. Brig. Gen. Wm. Morris, 2nd U.S. Artillery	June-July	1862
[Monthly Post Returns Unavailable	August	1862–
	November	1862]
Brig. Gen. Wm. W. Morris, 2nd U.S. Artillery	December	1862–
	July	1863
Lt. Col. Edward Murray, 5th NY Artillery	August	1863
Col. Peter A. Porter, 8th NY Artillery	September-December	1863
Lt. Col. William W. Bates, 8th NY Artillery	January-February	1864
Maj. James H. Willet, 8th NY Artillery	March	1864
Lt. Col. William W. Bates, 8th NY Artillery	April	1864
Brig. Gen. Wm. W. Morris, 2nd U.S. Artillery	May-September	1864
[Monthly Post Returns Unavailable	October	1864–
	February	1865]
Col. Daniel McCauley, 11th Indiana Veterans	March-April	1865
Maj. John F. Mount, 7th NY Artillery	May	1865

APPENDIX
E

$\mathcal{C}$IVIL WAR SITES IN BALTIMORE

*M*any of the structures that were an integral part of Baltimore during the Civil War no longer survive — however some have. The following lists those sites with their nineteenth century addresses. (Street numbers were changed in 1887). In addition are listed forty-four known forts, camps and redoubts constructed during the war, making Baltimore one of the most heavily fortified cities during that era.

RAILROAD STATIONS

Calvert Street Station (1848-1948) Northern Central Railroad
Location: Calvert and Centre Streets, Baltimore City. Present site of
            the Sunpapers building. Formerly the Baltimore and
            Susquehanna Railroad. Southern terminal of the Northern
            Central Railroad.
Notes: A medical and relief center during the Gettysburg cam-
            paign. Lincoln's funeral train departed here on April 21,
            1865. A portion of the rail bed is still utilized as the
            Baltimore Light Rail along Jones Falls, and from Monkton
            Station to the Pennsylvania line, as a popular 22 mile foot
            and bicycle path, maintained by the Maryland State Park
            Service.

Camden Street Station (1857-Restored 1993) Baltimore and Ohio Railroad
Location: Camden and Howard Streets. Present site of Oriole Park at
            Camden Yards, Baltimore City.
Notes: Lincoln passed through here for his inauguration in
            February 1861; November 18, 1863, to Gettysburg; April
            17, 1864, to address the Sanitary Fair in Baltimore; and on
            April 21, 1865, as his funeral train arrived from
            Washington.

President Street Station (1852-Restored 1997) Philadelphia, Wilmington & Baltimore Railroad
Location: President, Aliceianna and Fleet Streets, Baltimore City.
Notes: Southern terminal for the Philadelphia, Wilmington and
            Baltimore Railroad. Lincoln secretly passed through here
            on February 23, 1861, on his way to Washington. Pratt
            Street Riot began here on April 19, 1861. It ceased passen-
            ger service in 1873 when a new station opened on Charles
            Street (Pennsylvania Station). In April 1997 it reopened
            as a Civil War, Transportation, and Underground Railroad
            Museum.

Relay (1828 -1890) Baltimore and Ohio Railroad
Location: Relay, Baltimore County. Eight miles west of Baltimore
            adjacent to Patapsco River State Park.
Notes: Junction of the Baltimore and Ohio Railroad to Harpers

Ferry and Washington, D.C. The line is currently used as a freight line.

Baltimore and Ohio Railroad Coal Depot (1848 -19 —)

Location: Locust Point, bounded by Nicholson, Towson and Marriot Streets, Baltimore City.
Notes: Spur-line from Camden Street Station. Adjacent to Camp Cadwalander.

Mount Clare Station (1829-Present) Baltimore and Ohio Railroad

Location: Bounded by Pratt, Carey, McHenry and Poppleton Streets, Baltimore City.
Notes: Northern Terminal of the Baltimore and Ohio Railroad with connection to the Camden Street Station. Presently the Baltimore and Ohio Railroad Museum.

Bolton Street Station - Northern Central Railroad

Location: Bounded by Dolphin and Cathedral Streets, Baltimore City.
Notes: Southern terminal for the Northern Central Railroad. Also known as the Susquehanna Railroad Depot. On April 18, 1861, the Twenty-fifth Pennsylvania Infantry disembarked here and marched to Mount Clare Station, the first federal troops to respond to Lincoln's call for volunteers to protect the Capital.

Ellicott City Station (1831 - Present) Baltimore and Ohio Railroad

Location: Ellicott City, Baltimore County.
Notes: The oldest rail station in the world.

Monkton Station - Northern Central Railroad

Location: Route 138, Baltimore County.
Notes: Today the station and several buildings and rail bed are maintained as a 22 mile foot and bicycle path maintained by the Maryland State Park Service.

Magnolia Station - Philadelphia, Wilmington and Baltimore Railroad

Location: Bush River, Harford County.

Notes: In July 1864, Colonel Harry Gilmor, C.S.A.; captured Major General William B. Franklin, U.S.A., after burning the train he was on and the Bush River bridge.

Relay Station - Northern Central Railroad
Location: Bare Hills, Railroad Avenue. Lake Roland, Baltimore City.
Notes: Junction of the Northern Central Railroad and Western Maryland Railroad.

RAIL AND ROAD BRIDGES

Like the railroad, bridges that carried rail-lines and roads were protected by redoubts or camps, guarded by various federal troops.

Thomas Viaduct (1835-Present) Baltimore and Ohio Railroad
Location: Relay, Baltimore County.
Notes: Named for Philip E. Thomas, first President of the Baltimore and Ohio Railroad. Carried the line across the Patapsco River. The Thomas Viaduct is the only stone arch bridge built on a curve in the world. Length is 612 feet with eight elliptical arches which supported the 60 foot high structure. Benjamin Latrobe designed it and was built by John McCartney.
        Nearby is a monument erected by McCartney, listing the names of government and railroad officials.

Carrollton Viaduct (1829-Present) Baltimore and Ohio Railroad
Location: Washington Boulevard, adjacent to Carroll Park Golf course, Baltimore City.
Notes: Oldest stone railroad bridge in the United States. Carries the line across the Gwynns Falls.

Oliver Viaduct (1831-Present) Baltimore and Ohio Railroad
Location: Ellicott City Railroad Station, Baltimore County.
Notes: Passes over the National Road (U.S. Route 40).

Curtis Creek Bridge (unknown) Philadelphia, Wilmington and Baltimore Railroad
Location: Curtis Creek, Baltimore City.
Notes: Carried the PW&B into President Street Station. Burned

on April 20, 1861, to prevent passage of Northern troops into Baltimore.

Sweitzer's Bridge (unknown) Annapolis Road
Location: West Branch of the Patapsco River, Anne Arundel County.
Notes: Carried the Annapolis Road across the Ferry Branch.

Washington Turnpike Bridge (unknown)
Location: Elkridge Landing. Relay, Baltimore County.
Notes: Carried the Baltimore-Washington Road to the Capital. Site now is U.S. Route 1.

Long Bridge (unknown) Fairfield Road
Location: Ferry Branch of the Patapsco River, Baltimore City.
Notes: Carried a road from Ferry Point to the U.S. Marine Hospital located in Fairfield.

PUBLISHING HOUSES

There were numerous Baltimore City papers, many of ethnic readerships. Those listed were the major papers available during the war. Only *The Sun* remains in print today.

The Sun (1837-Present)
Location: SE corner of Baltimore and South Streets.
Publisher: Arunah B. Abel.
Notes: The Sun Iron building, as it was known, was built in 1850. Demolished in the 1904 fire. One of the few major papers not suspended during the war. It is the oldest continuous daily published in Baltimore.

Catholic Mirror (18— -1863)
Location: 174 W. Baltimore Street.
Publisher: Michael J. Kelly and John B. Piet.
Notes: On September 29, 1863, both men were arrested and the Mirror was suspended for printing and selling Frank Key Howard's pamphlet Fourteen Months in American Bastiles in 1863.

Daily Exchange (1858-1861)

Location: Baltimore and North Streets.
Publisher: Charles G. Kerr and Thomas W. Hall (Proprietor).
Notes: Founded and issued its first edition on February 22, 1858. Paper was joined in 1860 by William W. Glenn, Frank Key Howard and William Carpenter. In 1861, espousing "Southern Rights" the paper was suspended on September 14, 1861, with Glenn, Howard, and Hall being confined at Fort McHenry. The paper evolved during the war into the Maryland Times, Maryland News Sheet, and the Baltimore Daily Gazette.

Maryland Times (September 19 - September 23, 1861)

Location: Unknown.
Publisher: Edward F. Carter and William H. Neilson.
Notes: Four issues were published.

Maryland News Sheet (September 24, 1861 - August 14, 1862)

Location: Unknown.
Publisher: William Neilson (compositor), Edward F. Carter (manager), and William H. Carpenter (editor).
Notes: Paper was suppressed on August 14. Both Neilson and Carpenter were confined at Fort McHenry. Carter left for Canada.

Baltimore Daily Gazette (October 6, 1862 - September 29, 1863)

Location: Unknown.
Publisher: William Neilson and Edward F. Carter.
Notes: Carter having returned from Canada was arrested.

Baltimore and American Daily Advertiser (17— -198-)

Location: 28 W. Baltimore Street.
Publisher: Charles Fulton.
Notes: On June 29, 1861, Fulton was confined at Fort McHenry. The paper remained in circulation throughout the war. Later renamed the Baltimore News American.

E. Sachse and Company (1861-   )

Location: 104 S. Charles Street.
Publisher: Edward Sachse.

Notes: Lithograph artisans provided detailed scenes of camps and forts of Baltimore during the war, offering for purchase by soldiers for one dollar as souvenirs.

Baltimore Republican (18— -1863)
Location: 72 Baltimore Street.
Publisher: Beale and Francis Richardson, and Stephen J. Joyce.
Notes: On September 11, 1863, the paper was suspended for publishing a poem by Mrs. Ellen Key Blunt entitled "The Southern Cross."

Baltimore Evening News (18— -1863)
Location: Unknown.
Publisher: James R. Brewer, Editor.
Notes: On September 11, 1863, the paper was suspended with Brewer confined at Fort McHenry. Soon after it resumed publication, but on May 18, 1864, the paper was suspended for the remainder of the war.

Evening Transcript (1863-May 1864)
Location: Unknown.
Publisher: William H. Neilson.
Notes: First edition appeared on October 26, 1863, until suspended on November 10, 1863. It resumed shortly thereafter until finally suppressed on May 18, 1864.

The South (April 22, 1861 - February 17, 1862)
Location: 122 W. Baltimore Street (1861).
Publisher: Thomas W. Hall, Editor.
Notes: Perhaps the most radical Southern paper in Baltimore, "devoted to the South, Southern rights, and Secession." Paper was suspended on September 19, 1861. Hall was confined at Fort McHenry and later Fort Warren. Resumed publication on September 19 and continued until February 17, 1862, when its new editor, John M. Mills, was also confined at Fort McHenry.

FEDERAL HOSPITALS

The following medical facilities were used during the war to care and treat thousands of Confederate and Union soldiers who were conveyed to Baltimore from the various campaigns. Many were converted from former military camps.

U.S. Army General Hospital, Wests Buildings
Name: Owner James Wests.
Location: Union Dock, foot of Jones Falls, Baltimore City.
Notes: Consisted of six large warehouses. Converted in 1862 with 425 beds. Destroyed by the Baltimore fire in 1904.

U.S. Army General Hospital, McKim's Mansion
Name: Former home of John McKim. Property of George R. Vickers.
Location: South of Greenmount Cemetery, bounded by Preston, Valley, Chase and Homewood Avenues. See Camp McKim, Fort No. 8.
Notes: Former military camp. By 1862 barracks converted to 200 bedsteads. Sold at public auction in November 1865. Became Johnson Square in 1878.

U.S. Army General Hospital, Jarvis - Steuart Mansion Hospital
Name: Dr. Nathan S. Jarvis, Medical Director of Maryland.
Location: West of Fulton Avenue between W. Fayette and W. Baltimore Streets.
Notes: Formerly Steuart Mansion Hospital upon the estate of General George H. Steuart, C.S.A. Established on June 20,1862 with 600 bedsteads. By 1864 had a capacity of 1,500 bedsteads. Adjacent to Camp Simpson. Buildings sold at auction in May 1866.

U.S. Army General Hospital, Camden Hall, National Hotel, and Adams House
Name: Camden Station of the Baltimore and Ohio Railroad.
Location: Northside of the Camden Street Station.
Notes: One of the first hospitals established in 1861 because of its close proximity to the Camden Street Station. Capacity of 500 bedsteads. Closed June 1865.

U.S. Army General Hospital, Hicks.
Name: Maryland Governor Thomas Hicks.
Location: NW Baltimore City. Lafayette and Pulaski Streets, near St. Peter's Roman Catholic Cemetery.
Notes: Established June 9, 1865. Closed June 1866.

U.S. Army General Hospital, Newton University
Name: Newton University.
Location: Northside of Lexington Street, near Calvert and North
            Streets.
Notes: Established in 1862, with 1,200 bedsteads. Demolished in
            1867 for present day Baltimore City Hall on Holliday
            Street. Closed June 1865.

U.S. Army General Hospital, Patterson Park
Name: William Patterson who donated land as a public park in
            1827.
Location: Patterson Park, Baltimore City.
Notes: Former Hampstead Hill in 1814. Earthworks from War of
            1812 still present at the time. Established as a hospital in
            1862 with 1,300 bedsteads. Closed June 5, 1865.
            See also Camp Washburn-Patterson, Fort No. 12.

U.S. Marine Hospital
Name: Established as same in 1847.
Location: Fairfield, Anne Arundel County. Across the Ferry Branch
            from Fort McHenry.
Notes: Originally a city smallpox hospital. In 1848 the name
            changed to Marine Hospital.

Fort McHenry Post Hospital
Name: James McHenry, Secretary of War-1800.
Location: Grounds of Fort McHenry, Baltimore City.
Notes: Since 1814 a federal hospital was located on the military
            grounds. A newer hospital was erected adjacent to main
            gate. In July 1863, Major General James L. Kemper,
            C.S.A, and Major General Isaac R. Trimble, C.S.A., were
            treated here, following the Battle of Gettysburg.

Baltimore Dispensary
Name: Established as same in c.1830.
Location: University of Maryland Medical Complex, Baltimore City.
Notes: Became a part of the University after the war.

Church Home and Hospital
Name: Established as same in 1858.
Location: Broadway in East Baltimore, north of Fells Point,
            Baltimore City.

Notes: Private Episcopal Church facility. In 1849, writer Edgar
              Allan Poe died here.

MILITARY OFFICES

Numerous buildings in Baltimore were converted to military offices during the war for a variety of functions from recruiting rendezvous, commissary, quartermaster, and provost marshal offices. Here are a few of the
most prominent offices.

Federal Recruiting Office
Location: 112 W. Baltimore Street, Baltimore City.
Notes: One of several recruiting stations for the federal army.

Provost Marshal Offices and Prison - Gilmor House
Location: 24 Fayette Street, Battle Monument Square, Baltimore
              City.
Notes: This 150 room building, also known as the St. Clair and
              Guy's Hotel was closed by the military during the war. It
              was utilized as a prison and office for the Provost Marshal.

Headquarters, Eighth Army Corps - Reverdy Johnson House (1780-1893)
Location: Fayette and Calvert Street, Battle Monument Square,
              Baltimore City.
Notes: Former residence of Senator Reverdy Johnson who later
              defended General Fitz John Porter and Mary Surratt.

Eutaw House (1836-1912)
Location: NW corner of Eutaw and West Baltimore Streets,
              Baltimore City.
Notes: Established in 1836 as a hotel. On December 4, 1861,
              General George B. McClellan dined here before proceed-
              ing northward on the Northern Central. In September
              1862, Brigadier General John R. Kenly, established his
              headquarters for the Maryland Brigade. In 1864, General
              Lew Wallace, commander of the Middle Department, 8th
              Army Corps established his headquarters here. On April
              11, 1865, Vice-Admiral David Farragut, the "Hero of
              Mobile Bay" made an address here during his visit.

Pikesville Arsenal

Location: Reisterstown Road, Pikesville, Baltimore County.
Notes: Established during the War of 1812. In June 1888, it
             became a home for Confederate Soldiers. It closed in 1932.
             Today it is occupied by the Maryland State Police.

U.S. Military Telegraph Office

Location: 24 Holliday Street, Baltimore City.
Notes: Established in 1862. In 1864 it served as a recruiting office
             for the U.S. Colored Troops.

PUBLIC BUILDINGS, CLUBS

Barnum's City Hotel (1825-1890)

Location: SW corner of Fayette and N. Calvert Streets, Battle
             Monument Square, Baltimore City.
Notes: One of the best known hotels in America during the nine-
             teenth century, was owned and operated by David Barnum.
             Here the suspected plot to assassinate President-elect
             Lincoln in February 1861 may have taken place. Present
             site of the Maryland Equitable building.

Maryland Institute Hall (1851-1904)

Location: Central Market and Baltimore Streets., Baltimore City.
Notes: President Lincoln addressed the U.S. Sanitary Fair here on
             April 18, 1864, for the benefit of the U.S. Sanitary and
             Christian Commission. Presidents Franklin Pierce and
             Williard Fillmore were nominated here.

Battle Monument Square (1815-Present)

Location: Calvert and Lexington Streets, Baltimore City.
Notes: Designed by Maximilian Godefrey in 1815 as a monument
             to the 1814 defenders of Fort McHenry and the Battle of
             North Point. The monument is the official emblem of the
             City of Baltimore. On July 28, 1862, a Union rally for the
             draft was held here in which Governor Augustus W.
             Bradford gave a speech.

Maryland Union Commission

Location: 91 W. Baltimore Street, Baltimore City.
Notes: Established on April 18, 1865, to cooperate with the peo-
             ple of the South.

Union Club of Maryland

Location: 51 N. Charles Street, Baltimore City.

Notes: A popular social and political club founded in May 1863
            for the purpose of promoting "unqualified loyalty to the
            Government of the United States." Thomas H. Morris and
            Jerome N. Bonaparte were presidents. Among the 125
            members who met monthly were Enoch Pratt and John
            Hopkins.

Maryland Club (1820-1907)

Location: NE corner of Cathedral and Franklin Streets, Baltimore
            City.

Notes: Served as the Maryland Club from 1858 to 1863 when
            General Robert Schenck closed it down. On November
            11, 1864, General Lew Wallace established a Freedman's
            Bureau here to aid recently freed slaves and provide hous-
            ing for the sick and homeless in Maryland. It became
            known as "Freedman's Rest." After the war the site
            resumed as the Maryland Club until 1891. In 1907 it was
            torn down.

Old Masonic Hall (1814-1895)

Location: NE corner of St. Paul and Lexington Streets, Baltimore
            City.

Notes: Designed by Maximilian Godefrey, it became a federal
            courthouse in 1822. Here in June 1861, Chief Justice
            Roger B. Taney issued a writ of habeas corpus that was
            denied at the gates of Fort McHenry.

Baltimore Merchant Exchange - Old Custom House (1819-1902)

Location: NW corner of Gay and Lombard Streets, Baltimore City.

Notes: Designed by Benjamin Latrobe, it was here that President
            Lincoln's body lay in state on April 21, 1865, and was
            viewed by 10,000 citizens.

City Hall (1813-Present)

Location: N. Holliday Street, Baltimore City.

Notes: Built in 1813 as a public art and science museum by
            Rembrandt Peale. During the war it served as City Hall
            until the present city hall was erected in 1875 across the

street. Today, The Peale Museum and City Life Museums, occupy the site.

Douglass Institute (18— - Present)
Location: 210 Lexington Street, Baltimore City.
Notes: Established on May 19, 1870, it was originally part of the Newton University Hospital complex. On May 19, 1870, it became known as the Douglass Institute where Frederick Douglass gave an oration that day following a parade of African-American citizens.

Taylor's Hall
Location: Fayette and Calvert Streets, Baltimore City.
Notes: Headquarters of the States Rights Club. Here on April 18, 1861, the States Rights Convention was held to protest Lincoln's April 15 proclamation for federal troops to defend Washington.

U.S. Christian Commission
Location: 77 W. Baltimore Street, Baltimore City.
Notes: Established on May 4, 1861, to "afford both physical and spiritual aid to the sick and wounded soldiers as well as to disseminate religious truth among military camps and hospitals.

Front Street Theatre (1829-1838-1904)
Location: NW corner of Front and Low Streets, Baltimore City.
Notes: Douglas was nominated here in this 4,000 seat auditorium in 1861. On June 7-8, 1864, the Union National Convention was held here to nominate a candidate for presidency and vice-presidency of the United States. Lincoln was nominated in the first ballot.

Washington Monument (1830-Present)
Location: N. Charles and Monument Streets, Mount Vernon Square, Baltimore City.
Notes: The first official monument to George Washington. Its location in the Mount Vernon residential district became the center of the Southern secessionist movement in Baltimore. One of the 10-inch columbiads at Fort McHenry was pointed in this direction - three miles away!

Old Holliday Street Theatre (1813-1874)

Location: Holliday Street, Baltimore City.

Notes: A popular theater and the site where on October 17, 1814, "The Star- Spangled Banner" was first sung in public. Formerly a wooden structure in 1794, it was replaced in 1813 by a masonry structure. The site is now the War Memorial Plaza across the street from City Hall.

Ladies Union Relief Association of Baltimore

Location: 124 N. Howard Street (Oct. 1861) and 39 Lexington Street (Nov. 1861), Baltimore City.

Notes: Organization for the comfort and relief of the soldier.

Carroll Hall (c.1850 - c.1900)

Location: SE corner of Baltimore and Calvert Streets, Baltimore City.

Notes: A popular assembly room for military and political meetings.

CHURCHES

St. Lawrence Roman Catholic Chapel (1857-1887)

Location: East Fort Avenue and Towson Street, Locust Point, Baltimore City.

Notes: In April 1861, Captain John Robinson of Fort McHenry threatened to shell the city if any civilian militia came this side of the chapel. In 1887, the chapel was replaced with Our Lady of Good Counsel.

Light Street Methodist (Lovely Lane) (c.1796-c.1872)

Location: SW corner of Light Street and Wine Alley, Baltimore City.

Notes: The third meeting house of the founding church of American Methodism. In 1861, the Southern and Northern factions of the Methodist conference split into two separate entities here.

PRIVATE RESIDENCES

Mount Vernon Square

Location: N. Charles and Monument Streets, Baltimore City.

Notes: The most influential residential area of Baltimore during the war, became the center of Southern Secessionism in Baltimore. Site of the first official monument to George Washington in the country.

Albert Mansion (1850-Present)
Location: 700 N. Cathedral Street, Mount Vernon Square, Baltimore City.
Notes: The residence of William J. Albert, a leader of the German community and member of the Unconditional Union Party in Baltimore. President Lincoln spent the night here on April 18, 1864, following his speech at the Maryland Institute before the U.S. Sanitary and Christian Commission Fair. Today the house is occupied by the Agora Publishing Co.

Judge John Glenn (1859-Present)
Location: N. Charles and Madison Streets, Mount Vernon Square, Baltimore City.
Notes: The father of William W. Glenn, editor of pro-Southern paper *The Exchange*. Their summer home "Hilton" is located on the present site of Catonsville Community College, Catonsville, Baltimore County.

John S. Gittings (Present)
Location: Mount Vernon Square, Baltimore City.
Notes: Mr. Gittings was the President of the Northern Central Railroad. In February 1861, Mrs. Eleanor Gittings, a known Southern sympathizer, entertained Mrs. Lincoln and her sons here for a brief period as the Lincoln party made their perilous transit through Baltimore.

John W. Garrett (1860-1930)
Location: N. Charles and Madison Streets, Mount Vernon Square, Baltimore City.
Notes: Garrett was the President of the Baltimore and Ohio Railroad, a strong Union supporter during the war.

Robert Edward Lee (1846-1957)
Location: 908 Madison Street, Baltimore City.
Notes: The home of Robert E. Lee while with the U.S. Army

Corps of Engineers during the construction of Fort Carroll (1848-1852). While here he attended the mount Cavalry Episcopal Church. In 1852, Lee was appointed Superintendent of the U.S. Military Academy at West Point.

"Montevideo" Governor Augustus Bradford

Location: N. Charles Street and Lake Avenue, Baltimore City.
Notes: House was burned by the First Maryland Cavalry, C.S.A., on July 10, 1864, under General Bradley T. Johnson in retaliation for Governor Lechner of Virginia's home being burned by union troops. Site occupied by the Elkridge Club.

Hampton Mansion (1790-Present)

Location: Hampton Lane, Towson, Baltimore County.
Notes: The estate of the Ridgely Family from 1790 to 1948. In January 1861, under the state militia laws, Captain Charles Ridgely organized the Baltimore County Horse Guards, a company of "states' rights gentlemen." John Merryman, of "Ex parte Merryman" served as a lieutenant in the company. The site was established as a National Historic Site, National Park Service.

"Hayfields" Home of John Merryman (1805-Present)

Location"   Cockeysville, Baltimore County.
Notes: On the night of April 25, 1861, federal troops arrested Merryman and imprisoned him at Fort McHenry. He had participated in burning the rail bridges the day after the Pratt Street Riot on April 19. As a result of the political arrest, it placed President Lincoln and Chief Justice Roger Taney in a celebrated case of "Merryman vs. the United States."

Tudor Hall (Present)

Location: Bel Air, Harford County.
Notes: Birthplace and childhood home of actor John Wilkes Booth. A private residence today.

Ross Winans, "Crimea"

Location: Leakin Park, Baltimore City.
Notes: In 1843, Ross Winans (1796-1877), an engineer-industrial-

ist, was asked to provide the rolling stock for the St. Petersburg-to-Moscow rail line. Winans sent his sons, Thomas and William, to build the first major railroad in Russia. The Russian Czar awarded the family for their efforts, several million dollars, enabling them to build a lavish 1,000 acres estate, that is today Leakin Park. During the Civil War Ross Winans, a locomotive designer for the B&O Railroad, was arrested twice as an active Southern sympathizer, manufacturing pikes, as well as being a delegate from Baltimore City. Behind his mansion he constructed what became known as "Winan's Fort," an earthen defensive redoubt.

CEMETERIES

Greenmount Cemetery (1838-Present)
Location: Greenmount and North Avenues, Baltimore City.
Notes: Among the well known Civil War personages buried here are: John Wilkes Booth, Joseph E. Johnston, C.S.A., Erastus B. Tyler, U.S.A., John R. Kenly, U.S.A., Lewis H. Little, C.S.A., Benjamin Hugher, C.S.A., and George Hume Steuart, C.S.A., and Governor Augustus W. Bradford.

Old St. Paul's Cemetery (c.1750-Present)
Location: West Redwood Street, University of Maryland Hospital, Baltimore City.
Notes: The oldest cemetery in Baltimore where many notable military and civilians lie. Among them are Lewis Addison Armistead, C.S.A., his uncle George Armistead, U.S.A., commander of Fort McHenry during the War of 1812.

Loudon Park Cemetery (1853-Present)
Location: Frederick Road, Baltimore City.
Notes: The largest cemetery in Baltimore contains the graves of some 2,300 Union and 650 Confederate soldiers. Among those buried on "Confederate Hill" are Bradley T. Johnston, C.S.A., and Harry Gilmor, C.S.A. The last Civil War soldier buried here was on August 17, 1937.

Loudon National Cemetery (1861-Present)

Location: Frederick Road, Baltimore City.

Notes: In December 1861, the U.S. Sanitary Commission selected a section of the Loudon Park Cemetery. It became known as the "Government Lot." Here twenty-nine Union and Confederate soldiers, once buried at Fort McHenry were finally laid to rest in 1895. Site of Union Unknown Soldier's Monument.

Fort McHenry Post Cemetery (c.1790 -1852-1895)

Location: Fort McHenry National Monument, Baltimore City.

Notes: Confederate and Union remains and those soldiers who once served here were removed in June 1895 to Loudon National Cemetery and other sites.

SHIPYARDS

During the war Baltimore contained numerous shipyards which had government contracts, from building warships to providing supply and troop transports.

A. W. Denmead & Son Shipyard

Location: Foot of Lakewood Avenue, Canton, Baltimore City.

Notes: The USS *Monocacy*, a 1,370 ton light draft side-wheel steamer, iron- double ender gunboat was launched on December 14, 1864. Cost: $275,000. On May 4, 1865, the USS *Waxsaw*, a monitor, was launched here.

William Skinner & Sons Shipyard (1845-1906)

Location: Base of Federal Hill, Baltimore City.

Notes: Repair facility of steamboats for the Union navy.

Thomas H. Booz & Brothers (1848-   )

Location: On Harris Creek, at the foot of Kenwood Avenue, Canton, Baltimore City.

Notes: In November 1861, the firm received contracts for building pontoon bridges for the army.

John J. Abrahams and Ashcroft Shipyard

Location: Corner of Thames and Wolfe Streets, Fells Point, Baltimore City.

Notes: On October 3, 1861, the U.S. Gunboat *Pinola* was launched. The former New York steam ferry boat *Ethan Allen*, used as a troop and supply transport, was refitted here in November 1861.

IRON-WORKS

Horace Abbott and Sons
Location: Canton, Baltimore City.
Notes: Provided armor plating for the USS *Monitor* and other iron-clads. Mill No. 2 contained three heating and two pudding furnaces and one pair of 10- foot rolls, the largest in the country. The Abbott and the Tredegar ironworks in Richmond were the largest in the South.

Charles Reeder Works (1825-1904)
Location: Hughes Street between Battery Avenue and Henry Street, Federal Hill, Baltimore City.
Notes: Provided the machinery works for the U.S. Gunboat Pinola and other vessels during the war.

FORTS, REDOUBTS AND CAMPS

By the autumn of 1864, forty-four known forts, redoubts, and camps encircled Baltimore guarding vital communication lines. Due to the absence of monthly reports, it is impossible to be certain of all the camp sites and units who served in Baltimore. Those that are documented are listed to show the variety of state and federal regiments that served. While a numbered regiment is listed, these consisted of one or more companies, serving for various lengths of service.

Sources: "Returns of U.S. Military Posts," M-617 and "U.S. Army Corps of Engineers Military Maps," Record Group 77, National Archives; regimental histories, and reliable newspaper sources.

Fort McHenry
Name: Named for Secretary of War James McHenry in 1797.
Established: "An act to provide for the defense of certain ports and harbors of the United States," February 20, 1794.
Location: Locust Point, Baltimore City.
Armament: 72 guns. See Chapter 5: "Armament."

Units:	U.S. Marines (detachment)	1861
	1st U.S. Artillery	1861
	2nd U.S. Artillery	1861–1865
	4th U.S. Artillery	1861–1865
	5th U.S. Infantry	1861
	1st U.S. Infantry	1861
	U.S.S. *Allegheny* (80 sailors)	1864
	18th Connecticut Infantry	1861, 1863
	3rd Massachusetts Infantry	1861, 1864
	3rd New York Infantry	1861–1862
	4th New York Infantry	1862
	12th New York Infantry	1862
	19th New York Infantry	1862
	47th New York Infantry	1862
	6th New York Artillery	1862–1863
	5th New York Artillery	1863
	55th New York National Guard	1863
	21st New York Infantry	1863
	Baltimore Light Artillery	1863
	17th New York Infantry	1863
	1st Pennsylvania Artillery	1863
	3rd Pennsylvania Artillery	1863
	8th New York Artillery	1863–1864
	5th Massachusetts Infantry	1864
	192nd Pennsylvania Infantry	1864
	131st Ohio National Guard Infantry	1864
	137th Ohio National Guard Infantry	1864
	144th Ohio National Guard Infantry	1864
	149th Ohio National Guard Infantry	1864
	91st New York Veteran Infantry	1864–1865
	7th New York Artillery	1865
	11th Indiana Veteran Infantry	1865

Fort Federal Hill (Fort No. 15)

Name: In 1789, when Marylanders ratified the Federal Constitution. Previously known as Observatory Hill and Captain John Smith Hill.

Location: Federal Hill, Baltimore City.

Armament: (1864) Five 10-inch S.C. mortars, two 8-inch S.C. mortars, five 24 pounders, six 8-inch columbiads, twenty-three 32 pounders, and six 6 pounders.

Units:	5th Indiana Infantry	1861
	1st Pennsylvania Infantry	1861
	18th Pennsylvania Infantry	1861
	5th New York Infantry	1861–1862
	3rd New York Infantry	1862
	7th New York National Guard	1862
	8th New York Artillery	1862–1864
	55th New York Infantry	1863
	69th New York Infantry	1863
	5th Massachusetts Infantry	1864
	7th New York Infantry	1864
	131st Ohio National Guard	1864
	144th Ohio National Guard	1864

Fort Marshall (Fort No. 14)

Name: Colonel Thomas H. Marshall, Seventh Maine Infantry. Died October 25, 1861.
- Potters Hill (Race Course)
- Murray's Hill

Established: 1861.

Location: Site of Sacred Heart Catholic Church in Highlandtown, Baltimore City.

Armament: Sixty guns.

Units:	7th Maine Infantry	1861
	18th Connecticut Infantry	1861
	17th Massachusetts Infantry	1862
	17th Connecticut Infantry	1862
	5th New York Artillery	1862–1864
	5th New York Infantry	1862
	19th New York Artillery	1862
	3rd New York Infantry	1862
	69th New York Infantry	1863
	8th New York Artillery	1863
	5th Massachusetts Infantry	1864
	131st Ohio National Guard Infantry	1864
	137th Ohio National Guard Infantry	1864
	144th Ohio National Guard Infantry	1864

Fort Carroll

Name: Charles Carroll of Carrollton, Maryland signer of the Declaration of Independence.

Established: 1848.
Location: Sollers Point, mid-channel, Patapsco River. Four miles
             below Fort McHenry.
Armament: Unknown.
Units: 5th U.S. Infantry   1861
            5th Massachusetts Infantry   1864

Camp Belger

Name: Colonel James W. Belger, Assistant Quartermaster, Middle
             Department, 1861–1863.
             - Smiths Woods
Established: 1862.
Location: Madison and North Avenues.
Armament: Unknown.
Units: Boston Light Artillery   1861
             6th Massachusetts Infantry   1861
             3rd Maryland Infantry   1861
             17th Massachusetts Infantry   1861
             21st Massachusetts Infantry   1861
             140th New York Infantry   1862
             114th New York Infantry   1862
             38th Massachusetts Infantry   1862
             37th New York National Guard   1862
             8th New York Artillery*   1862–1864
             7th U.S. Colored Troops   1863
             21st New York Infantry   1863
             150th New York Infantry   1863
             4th U.S. Colored Troops   1864
             39th U.S. Colored Troops   1864

* Formerly the 129th New York Infantry, December 1862.

Relay Junction / Fort Dix / Camp Essex / Camp Morgan

Name: Relay Station of the Baltimore and Ohio Railroad.
             Fort Dix - Major General John A. Dix.
             Camp Essex - Essex County, Massachusetts.
             Camp Morgan - unknown.
Established: 1861.
Location: Series of artillery redoubts protecting the Thomas Viaduct
             Bridge over the Patapsco River, Patapsco State Park.

Armament: Two 12-Pdr. Mountain Howitzers, One 24-Pdr. field gun, Three 10- Pdr. Parrott guns, Twenty 12-Pdr. James guns, and Two 8-inch Siege mortars.

Units:		
8th New York Artillery	1861	
6th Massachusetts Infantry	1861	
Boston Light Artillery	1861	
4th Wisconsin Infantry	1861	
60th New York Infantry	1861–1862	
8th Massachusetts Infantry	1861	
10th Maine Infantry	1861	
1st Maryland Infantry	1861	
5th New York Artillery	1862	
138th Pennsylvania Infantry	1862–1863	
118th New York Infantry	1862–1863	
11th Maryland Infantry	1864–1865	

Camp Cadwalader

Name: Major General George Cadwalader, Pennsylvania Volunteers.
- Locust Point
Established: 1861.
Location: Locust Point, adjacent to Fort McHenry, Baltimore City.
Armament: None.

Units:	
1st Pennsylvania Light Guards	1861
2nd Philadelphia National Guard	1861
19th Pennsylvania Infantry	1861
21st Indiana Infantry	1861
3rd New York Infantry	1861
60th New York Infantry	1861

Camp Andrew (Fort No. 1 1/2)

Name: Governor John A. Andrews of Massachusetts
- Steuart's Grove or Steuart's Woods after owner George H. Steuart.
- Camp Reynolds.
- Camp Creager, after Colonel J.P. Creager, First Maryland Independent Cavalry.
- Camp Wool, after Major General John E. Wool.
- Camp Simpson, after Major Marcus De LaFayette Simpson, Commissary Subsistence, Middle Department.
- Bellevue Gardens.

Established: 1861.
Location: Baltimore Street and Fulton Avenue, Baltimore City.
              Located on the estate of General George Hume Steuart,
              C.S.A. Site of present day Bon Secours Hospital.
Armament: Unknown.
Units:

7th Maine Infantry	1861
1st Maryland Regiment	1861
17th Massachusetts	1861–1862
2nd Massachusetts Artillery	1861
7th New York National Guard	1862
8th New York Artillery	1862
151st New York Infantry	1863
18th Connecticut Infantry	1863
72nd U.S. Veterans Reserve Corps	1864

Camp Carroll

Name: Charles Carroll, the Banister.
              - Camp Chesebrough, after Lt. Colonel William G.
              Chesebrough, 11th
                 U.S. Infantry.
Established: 1861.
Location: Carroll Park, Baltimore City.
Armament: None
Units:

1st Maryland Infantry	1861
13th New York Infantry	1861
4th Wisconsin Infantry	1861
8th Pennsylvania Infantry	1861
4th Pennsylvania Infantry	1861
4th Maryland Infantry	1861–1862
22nd Pennsylvania Infantry	1861
Boston Light Artillery	1861
Massachusetts Light Artillery	1861
17th Massachusetts Infantry	1861
2nd Maryland Infantry	1861
1st Pennsylvania Infantry	1861
7th New York Infantry	1861
13th Pennsylvania Cavalry	1862
1st Connecticut Cavalry	1863–1864
1st Maryland Veterans Cavalry	1864
11th Maryland Infantry	1864

Camp Washburn (Fort No. 12)

Name: Governor Israel Washburn of Maine.
              - Camp Patterson, after William Patterson, who in 1827
              donated the land   for a park.
Established: 1861.
Location: Patterson Park, Baltimore City.
Armament: Five guns.
Units: Patapsco Guard Infantry   1861
              3rd Maryland Infantry   1861
              1st Pennsylvania Infantry   1861
              22nd Pennsylvania Infantry   1861
              6th Wisconsin Infantry   1861
              4th Wisconsin Infantry   1861
              7th Maine Infantry   1861
              10th Maine Infantry   1861
              20th New York Infantry   1861
              21st Massachusetts Infantry   1861
              10th New York Cavalry   1862
              19th Pennsylvania National Guard   1862
              110th New York Infantry   1862

Camp Druid Hill Park (Fort No. 5)

Name: Baltimore City Park.
Established: 1861.
Location: Druid Hill Park, Baltimore City.
Armament: Three guns.
Units: 1st Pennsylvania Infantry   1861
              21st Indiana Infantry   1861
              37th New York Infantry   1861
              7th Maryland Infantry   1862
              8th New York Heavy Artillery   1864

Camp McKims (Fort No. 8)

Name: John McKim, estate owner.
Established: 1861.
Location: South of Greenmount Cemetery, bounded by Preston,
              Chase and Homewood Streets, Baltimore City.
Armament: Three field guns.
Units: 5th Wisconsin Infantry   1861
              13th New York Infantry   1861
              6th Michigan Infantry   1861

6th Maine Infantry	1861
16th Massachusetts Infantry	1861
87th Pennsylvania Infantry	1862
8th New York Heavy Artillery	1864

Fort Worthington (Fort No. 13)

Name: Believed to be Henry G. Worthington, born in Cumberland, Maryland, who served as U.S. Representative from Nevada, 1864–1865.

Established: 1864.

Location: Kenwood and Preston Streets, south of Baltimore Cemetery, Baltimore City.

Armament: Eight field guns.

Units:		
	8th New York Heavy Artillery	1864
	11th Maryland Infantry	1864

Fort No. 1/2

Name: None.

Established: 1864.

Location: West Baltimore and Smallwood Streets, Baltimore City.

Armament: Unknown.

Fort No. 1

Name: None.

Established: 1863.

Location: West Baltimore Street, Baltimore City.

Armament: Twelve field guns.

Units:		
	5th New York Artillery	1863
	8th New York Heavy Artillery	1864

Fort No. 2

Name: None.

Established: 1864.

Location: NE corner of Franklin Street and Kirby's Lane, Baltimore City.

Armament: Unknown.

Unit:		
	8th New York Heavy Artillery	1864

Fort No. 3

Name: None.

Established: 1864.

Location: Gilmor and Townsend Streets, Baltimore City.
Armament: Three field guns.
Unit: 8th New York Heavy Artillery   1864

Fort No. 4

Name: None.
Established: 1864.
Location: Gilmor Street and Winsor Mill Road, Baltimore City.
Armament: Two field guns.
Unit: 8th New York Heavy Artillery   1864

Fort No. 4 1/2

Name: None.
Established: 1864.
Location: NE corner of Gilmor and Baker Streets, Baltimore City.
Armament: Three field guns.
Unit: 8th New York Heavy Artillery   1864

Fort No. 5 (See Camp Druid Hill Park)

Fort No. 6

Name: None.
Established: 1864.
Location: Unknown, Baltimore City.
Armament: Unknown.
Units: 19th U.S. Colored Troops   1864
        8th New York Heavy Artillery   1864

Fort No. 7

Name: None.
Established: 1864.
Location: Near Mount Royal Reservoir, adjacent to the Northern Central Railroad, Baltimore City.
Armament: Five field guns.
Units: [Baltimore] Union Club Company   1864
        19th U.S. Colored Troops   1864
        8th New York Heavy Artillery   1864

Fort No. 7 1/2

Name: None.
Established: 1864.

Location: Opposite Camp Bradford, North Charles Street, Baltimore City.
Armament: Six field guns.
Units: Unknown.

Fort No. 8 (See Camp McKim).

Fort No. 9
Name: None.
Established: 1864.
Location: Harford Road and North Avenue, Baltimore City.
Armament: Two field guns.
Unit: 8th New York Heavy Artillery   1864

Fort No. 10
Name: None.
Established: 1864.
Location: Caroline Street, Fells Point, Baltimore City.
Armament: Unknown.
Unit: 8th New York Heavy Artillery   1864

Fort No. 11
Name: None.
            - Fort Rosehill
Established: 1864.
Location: East Monument Street, near Johns Hopkins Hospital, Baltimore City.
Armament: Unknown.
Units: Unknown.

Fort No. 12   (See Camp Washburn).

Fort No. 13   (See Fort Worthington).

Fort No. 14   (See Fort Marshall).

Battery A
Name: None.
Established: 1864.
Location: NE corner of Monroe and Ramsey Streets, Baltimore City.

Armament: Unknown.
Units: Unknown.

Camp Hoffman
Name: Colonel William A. Hoffman, U.S. Commissioner of
             Prisoners.
Established: 1861.
Location: Arlington Avenue and Lanvale Street, LaFayette Square,
             Baltimore City.
Armament: Unknown.
Units: 5th Maryland Infantry   1861
             [Baltimore] Public Guard Regt.   1861
             5th New York Artillery   1862
             8th New York Heavy Artillery   1864

Camp Melvale
Name: Melvale, Maryland.
             - Camp Small, Charles W. Small, property owner.
Established: 1861.
Location: Cold Spring Lane and Jones Falls, Cross Keys, Baltimore
             City.
Armament: None.
Units: 87th Pennsylvania Infantry   1861–1862

Camp Chapin
Name: Colonel Edward P. Chapin, 116th New York Infantry.
Established: 1862.
Location: Druid Hill Park, Baltimore City.
Armament: None.
Unit: 116th New York Infantry   1862

Camp Cram
Name: Colonel Thomas Jefferson Cram, Chief, U.S.
             Topographical Engineers, Middle Department.
Established: 1862.
Location: Liberty Road near Powhattan Dam, NW Baltimore
             County.
Armament: Unknown.
Units: Unknown.

Camp Millington
Name: Unknown.

Established: 1862.
Location: East of Gwysnns Falls, Brunswick Street and Millington Avenue, adjacent to Camp Emory, Baltimore City.
Armament: Unknown.
Unit: 128th New York Infantry   1862

Camp Emory

Name: General William Hemsley Emory, U.S. Volunteers. A native Marylander.
Established: 1862.
Location: Adjacent to Camp Millington, Baltimore City.
Armament: Unknown.
Unit: 38th Massachusetts Infantry   1862

Camp Bradford

Name: Governor William Bradford of Maryland.
           - Camp Cattlegrounds, former State Agricultural Fairgrounds.
           - Camp Tyler.
Established: 1861. In 1864 the site became a hospital facility with 1,000 bedsteads.
Location: Between Charles and 26th Streets, Baltimore City.
Armament: Unknown.
Units: Independent Pennsylvania Cavalry   1861
           5th New York Infantry   1862
           Purnell Legion Cavalry   1862–1863
           8th New York Heavy Artillery   1864
           159th Ohio National Guard   1864

Camp Hay

Name: Unknown.
           - Camp Beaver. Colonel J.A. Beaver, 148th Pennsylvania Infantry.
Established: 1861.
Location: York Road and Sherwood Road, Cockeysville. One of several camps that guarded the Northern Central Railroad.
Armament: None.
Units: 1st Pennsylvania Infantry   1861
           12th Pennsylvania Infantry   1861
           20th Indiana Infantry   1861
           4th Wisconsin Infantry   1861

87th Pennsylvania Infantry	1862
2nd Maryland Eastern Shore Inf.	1862
148th Pennsylvania Infantry	1862

Camp Stansbury

Name: Located on the farm of C.S. Stansbury.
Established: 1861.
Location: Back River Bridge of the Baltimore, Wilmington and Philadelphia Railroad. Six miles from Baltimore on Moores Run in present day Rosedale, Baltimore County.
Armament: None.
Units:
  23rd Pennsylvania Infantry
  123rd Pennsylvania Infantry
  8th New York Cavalry
  10th New York Cavalry
  19th New York Infantry
  199th Ohio National Guard
  97th Ohio National Guard
  1st Delaware Infantry
  5th Delaware Infantry
  6th Delaware Infantry

Camp Seward

Name: Secretary of State William Seward.
Established: 1861.
Location: York Road at the Little Falls Bridge, Northern Central Railroad Bridge at Little Falls, Parkton, Baltimore County. One of several camps guarding the Northern Central Railroad.
Armament: None.
Unit: 140th Pennsylvania Infantry   1862

Camp Glory

Name: Unknown.
Established: 1861.
Location: Long Bridge, Ferry Branch, Patapsco River, SW Baltimore City.
Armament: None.
Unit: 8th New York Artillery   1862

Camp Donaldson
Name: Major James Lowry Donaldson, Chief Quartermaster, Middle Department.

A native Marylander.

Established: 1863.
Location: Unknown.
Armament: None.
Units: Unknown.

Camp Newport
Name: Captain Marshall Newport, Assistant Quartermaster, Middle Department.

Established: Unknown.
Location: Unknown.
Armament: None.
Units: Unknown.

Camp Meade
Name: Major General George G. Meade, U.S.A.
Established: 1863.
Location: North Charles Street, Baltimore City.
Armament: Unknown.
Units: Unknown.

ENDNOTES

Chapter 1

[1] Douglas S. Freeman, *R.E. Lee: A Biography*, (Charles Scribner's Sons: 1949), p. 305.

[2] Howard I. Chapelle, *The Baltimore Clipper*, (Dover Publications: 1988), p. 66.

[3] Ibid., p. 316.

[4] Eugene H. Roseboom, "Baltimore as a National Nominating Convention City," *Maryland Historical Magazine*, Vol. 67, No. 3, Fall 1972. p. 215. Hereafter cited as *MHM*.

[5] Ibid., p. 225.

[6] M. Halstead, *A History of the National Political Conventions*, (Follett, Foster, and Company: 1860), p.170.

[7] *MHM*, Fall 1972, pp. 248-249.

[8] Ibid., p. 259.

[9] Halstead, p. 120.

[10] Daniel C. Toomey, *The Civil War in Maryland*, (Toomey Press: 1983), p. 7.

Chapter 2

[1] Emerson D. Fite, *The Presidential Campaign of 1860*, (New York: 1911), p. 107. E.B. Long, *The Civil War Day by Day: An Almanac, 1861-1865*, (Doubleday and Company, Inc.: 1971), pp. 12-13.

[2] Lawrence M. Denton, *A Southern Star for Maryland*, (Publishing Concepts: 1995), p. 47-48.

[3] Ibid., p. 225.

[4] Earl S. Miers, Ed., *Lincoln Day by Day*, (Lincoln Sesquicentennial Commission: 1960), Vol. 3, p. 10; Harold R. Manakee, *Maryland in the Civil War*, (Maryland Historical Society: 1960), pp. 26-27.

[5] Norma B. Cuthbert, Ed., *Lincoln and the Baltimore Plot, 1861*, (The Huntington Library: 1949), p. 149; Isaac Markers, "Why President Lincoln Spared Three Lives," *The Confederate Veteran*, Vol. XIX, 1911, p. 382; "Selected Records Relating to Confederate Prisoners of War, 1861-1865," National Archives, M-

598, Roll 96 (Fort McHenry). Mrs. Gittings later served as a manager for the Southern Relief Fair held in Baltimore, April 2-13, 1866. The Gittings house still stands in Mount Vernon Square, Baltimore.

[6] Denton, pp. 47-49.

[7] William F. McKay, *Campfire Sketches and Battlefield Echoes of 61-65*, (Springfield: 1889), pp. 12-14.

[8] George W. Brown, *Baltimore and the 19th of April, 1861*, (Johns Hopkins University: 1887), p. 36; Matthew P. Andrews, "Passage of the Sixth Massachusetts through Baltimore, April 19, 1861," *MHM*, Vol. 19, No. 1, March 1919, pp. 65-67.

[9] *Baltimore American & Daily Advertiser* [Baltimore], April 1861.

[10] B.F. Watson, *Addresses, Reviews, and Episodes Chiefly concerning the "Old Sixth" Massachusetts Regiment*, (New York: 1901), pp. 19, 90.

[11] John W. Hanson, *Historical Sketch of the Old Sixth Regiment*, (Lee and Shepard: 1866), pp. 21-26.

[12] Brown, p. 46; *Official Records of the War of the Rebellion*, (G.P.O.: 1887), Series 1, Vol. 2, p. 7. Hereafter cited as *OR's*; Hanson, p. 25.

[13] Hanson, pp. 40-41; Watson, pp. 50-53.

[14] J. Thomas Scharf, *The Chronicles of Baltimore*, (Turnbull Brothers: 1874), pp. 591-592.

[15] Brown, pp. 49-51.

[16] Andrews, pp. 74-75; Brown, p. 49.

[17] Manakee, pp. 37-38.

[18] George L. Radcliff, *Governor Thomas H. Hicks of Maryland and the Civil War*, (The Johns Hopkins Press: 1901), p. 55.

[19] Radcliff, p. 56; Scharf, p. 596.

[20] Brown, pp. 64-65, 77; Scharf, pp. 599-601.

[21] John C. Robinson, "Baltimore in 1861," *The Magazine of American History*, Vol. 14, No. 3, September 1885, pp. 264-266. Robinson, a veteran of the Mexican War, later served in 1863, as a division commander in Reynold's I Corps at Oak Knoll, Gettysburg, Pa.

[22] J. M. Harris, *A Reminiscence of the Troubious Times of April, 1861*, (Baltimore: 1891), Maryland Historical Society Fund Publication No. 31, pp. 10-11, 18, 22.

[23] Charles McH. Howard, "Baltimore and the Crises of 1861," *MHM*, Vol. 41, No. 4, December 1946, pp. 261-262; Brown, pp. 65-66.

[24] Brown, p. 85; Radcliff, pp. 71-72.

Chapter 3

[1] *Official Records of the War of the Rebellion*, Series 1, Vol. 2, p. 207. Hereafter cited as *OR's*.

[2] Daniel C. Toomey, *A History of Relay, Maryland, and The Thomas Viaduct*, (Toomey Press: 1976), p. 15.

[3] Benjamin F. Butler, *Butler's Book*, (A. M. Thymer Co.: 1892), pp. 228-229.

[4] McHenry Howard, *Recollections of a Maryland Confederate Soldier and Staff Officer*, (William and Wilkins Co.: 1914), pp. 13-14.

[5] Daniel C. Toomey, *The Civil War in Maryland*, (Toomey Press: 1990, 4th Ed.), p. 19.

[6] *Harper's Weekly* (New York), June 8, 1861.

[7] General Winfield Scott (via Assistant Adj. Gen.) to Major George Cadwalader,

May 16, 1861. *OR's*, Series 2, Vol. 1, pp. 571-572. Cadwalader's rank was a brevet major- general.

8 "Executive Order in relation to State Prisoners, No 1," February 14, 1862. John A. Marshall, *American Bastile: A History of the Illegal Arrests and Imprisonment of American Citizens During the Late Civil War*, (Thomas W. Hartley, Printer, Philadelphia: 1870), pp. 717-718. The proclamation was issued by Secretary of War Edwin M. Stanton and signed by the President.

9 Mark E. Neely, *The Fate of Liberty: Abraham Lincoln and Civil Liberties*, (Oxford University Press: 1991), pp. 71-72.

10 Harold R. Manakee, *Maryland in the Civil War*, (Maryland Historical Society: 1961), p. 52; Walker Lewis, *Without Fear or Favor*, (Houghton Mifflin Co.: 1965), pp. 450- 452.

11 General George Cadwalader to Lt. Colonel E.D. Townsend, Asst. Adjt. Gen., May 25, 1861. *OR's*, Series 2, Vol. 1, p. 574.

12 H.H. Walker Lewis, "*Ex Parte* Merryman," MHM, Vol. 56, December 1961, p. 390.

13 Neely, p. 12.

14 Known as the Habeas Corpus Act of Congress, March 3, 1863. See Neely, pp. 68-69, 87.

15 *OR's*, Series 2, Vol. 1, p. 620

16 *The Sun* (Baltimore), July 6, 1861

Chapter 4

1 Sidney, T. Matthews, "Control of the Baltimore Press During the Civil War," *Maryland Historical Magazine* (Hereafter cited as MHM),Vol. 36, No. 2, June 1941, pp. 151, 153; Harold R. Manakee, *Maryland in the Civil War*, (Maryland Historical Society: 1961), pp. 44-45.

2 Manakee, p. 46.

3 *Baltimore American*, July 9, 10, 13, 1861; Charles A. Earp, "The Amazing Colonel Zarvona," MHM, Vol. 34, 1939, pp. 334-343.

4 Ibid.

5 Morgan Dix, *Memoirs of John Adams Dix*, (Harper & Brothers, New York: 1888), pp. 24-25.

6 Ibid., pp. 27-28.

7 *OR's*, Series 2, Vol. 1, pp. 678-679.

8 Lawrence Sangston, *The Bastiles of the North: By a Member of the Legislature*, (Baltimore: 1863), p. 8.

9 Major General John Dix to Major General George Cadwalader, September 5, 1861, *OR's*, Series 2, Vol. 1, p. 592.

10 Frank Key Howard, *Fourteen Months in American Bastiles*, (Kelly, Hedian & Piet: 1863), pp. 7-10.

11 Major General John Dix to Robert C. Winthrop, January 23, 1862. *OR's*, Series 2, Vol. 1, p. 617.

12 Commissioners H.L. Bond and John C. King to Edwin Stanton, September 30, 1864, *OR's*, Series 2, Vol. 7, pp. 898-899.

13 Major General John Dix to William Seward, February 17, 1862, *OR's*, Series 2, Vol. 2, pp. 226-228. Includes Colonel William Morris's "Report of political prisoners taken, released and remaining since March 4, 1861, at Fort McHenry,

Md.," February 16, 1862; "Abstracts from monthly returns of the principal U.S. military prisons," *OR's*, Series 2, Vol. 8, pp. 989-1002.

[14] Daniel D. Hartzler, *Marylanders in the Confederacy*, (Family Line Publications: 1986), p. 27.

[15] Charles Camper and J.W. Kirkley, *Historic Record of the First Maryland Infantry*, (Gibson Brothers: 1871), pp. 8-11.

[16] J. Thomas Scharf, *Chronicles of Baltimore*, (Turnbull Brothers: 1874), p. 616.

[17] Manakee, p. 58; J. Thomas Scharf, *History of Maryland*, Vol. 3, (Baltimore: 1879), p. 460.

[18] W. W. Goldsborough, *The Maryland Line in the Confederate Army, 1861-1865*, (Kennikat Press: 1972 edition), pp. 40-43; Camper and Kirkley, pp. 43-46.

[19] Scharf, *Chronicles*, p. 622.

[20] Ibid, pp. 623-624.

[21] George T. Ness, *The Regular Army on the Eve of the Civil War*, (Toomey Press: 1990), p. 29; Ezra J. Warner, *Generals in Blue*, (Louisiana State University Press: 1972), p. 573.

[22] *OR's*, Series 2, Vol. 4, p. 663; Charles B. Clark, "Suppression and Control of Maryland, 1861-1865," *MHM*, Vol. 54, No. 3, September 1959. p. 265.

[23] Camper and Kirkley, pp. 84-85.

[24] E.B. Long, *The Civil War Day by Day: An Almanac*, (Doubleday & Company, Inc: 1971), p. 270.

[25] Dr. Myron W. Robinson to parents, September 18, 1862. Personal Collection of Dr. S.J. Petrie. Photo-copy at Fort McHenry Library, National Park Service. Robinson served at the U.S. Army Convalescent Hospital at Fort McHenry.

[26] *The Sun* (Baltimore), August 20, 1862.

[27] *The Sun* (Baltimore), October 18, 1862.

[28] *The Sun* (Baltimore), December 1, 8, 1862.

[29] *The Sun* (Baltimore), October 18, 1862.

[30] Clark, pp. 268-269.

[31] Daniel C. Toomey, *The Civil War in Maryland*, (Toomey Press: 1990, 4th Ed.), p. 72.

[32] Appleton Annual Cyclopedia, Vol. 3, 1863), p. 615; Charles P. Clark, "Suppression and Control of Maryland, 1861-1865," *MHM*,

[33] Swinton, William A.M., *History of the Seventh Regiment National Guard*, (Fields, Osgood, & Co., 1870), pp. 299-301, 303, 306.

[34] William Swinton, *History of the Seventh Regiment, National Guard*, (Fields, Osgood, & Co. New York: 1870), pp. 313-316.

[35] Scharf, *History of Baltimore City and County*, p. 144.

[36] Swinton, p. 318; *The Sun* (Baltimore), July 6, 1863.

[37] Henry E. Shepard, *Narrative of Prison Life at Baltimore and Johnson's Island, Ohio*, (Baltimore: 1917), p. 6.

[38] Major General Robert C. Schenck to President Lincoln, July 11, 1863, *OR's*, Series, 2, Vol. 6, pp. 101- 102. For prisoner arrival estimates, see *The Sun* (Baltimore), July 1- 30, 1863; "Abstracts from monthly returns... for Fort McHenry, August 1863," *OR's*, Series, 2, Vol. 8, p. 991.

[39] Ibid.

[40] Kathy G. Harrison and John W. Busey, *Nothing But Glory: Pickett's Division at Gettysburg*, (Thomas Publications, Gettysburg: 1993), pp. 110-115. Lewis Armistead (1817-1863) was the son of Colonel Walker Keith Armistead, U.S. Army Corps of Engineers, brother of Lt. Colonel George Armistead (1780-1818) of Fort McHenry. Both are buried in the Hughes' family vault in St. Paul's Cemetery.

41 Clark, p. 266.

42 Scharf, *Chronicles*, p. 628.

43 *The Sun* (Baltimore), November 4, 1863.

44 Arch F. Blakey, General John H. Winder, C.S.A. (University of Florida Press: 1990), p. 150.

45 William I. Kelly, "Baltimore Steamboats in the Civil War," MHM, Vol. 37, No. 1, March 1942, p. 42.

46 Isaac M. Fein, "Baltimore Jews During the Civil War, " *American Jewish Historical Quarterly*, Vol. 51, No. 2, December 1961, pp. 87-88, 90.

47 L.J. Loudermilk, *History of the Cumberland*, (Washington: 1878), pp. 397-398; Warner, p. 535.

48 H.B. Smith, *Between the Lines*, (Booz Brothers: 1911), p. 80.

49 Toomey, *Civil War in Maryland*, p. 99.

50 Robert W. Schoeberlien, "A Fair to Remember," MHM, Vol. 90, No. 4, Winter 1995, pp. 471-473.

51 Mrs. Lincoln Phelps, Ed., *Our Country*, (Baltimore: 1864), Dedication page not numbered.

52 Miers, p. 253; Schoeberlien, pp. 477, 479.

53 *The Sun* (Baltimore), April 20, 1864.

54 Dieter Cunz, "The Maryland Germans in the Civil War," MHM, Vol. 36, No. 4, December 1941, p. 409; Schoeberlien, p. 482.

55 Scharf, *Chronicles*, p. 630.

56 Alfred S. Roe, *Monocacy*, (Toomey Press Edition, edited by Jerry Harlowe: 1996), pp. ix-x.

57 L.A. Wilmer, ed., *History and Roster of Maryland Volunteers, War of 1861-1865*, Volume 1, (Baltimore: 1898), p. 375; Milton A. Record, Guide Book and Descriptive Manual of Battle Flags...," (Baltimore: 1965), p. 217; OR's, Series 1, Vol. 37, Part 1, p.704.

58 Ulysses S. Grant, *Personal Memoirs*, (C.L. Webster Company: 1885), p. 305; Roe, p. 24.

59 Roe, pp. 21-23.

60 Scharf, *Chronicles*, p. 630.

61 Richard R. Duncan, "Maryland's Reaction to Early's Raid," MHM, Vol. 64, No. 3, Fall 1969, pp. 259-262.

62 Bradley T. Johnson, "My Ride Around Baltimore," *Southern Historical Society Papers*, Vol. 30, (Kraus Reprint: 1977), pp. 217-219.

63 Harry Gilmor, *Four Years in the Saddle* (Harper & Brothers: 1866), pp. 192-195.

64 Scharf, *Chronicles*, p. 630.

65 Toomey, *Civil War in Maryland*, p. 140; Scharf, Chronicles, pp. 631-632.

66 Smith, pp. 160-165.

67 Leo A. Knott, *Some Political Transactions in Maryland, 1861-1867 with a Biographical Sketch of A. Leo Knott*, (no date), pp. 18-19.

68 Toomey, *Civil War in Maryland*, pp. 141-142.

69 OR's, U.S. Navy Series 2, Vol. 1, p. 149.

70 Smith, pp. 206, 215-219.

71 Ibid., pp. 255-256, 258.

72 Scharf, *Chronicles*, p. 634.

73 Long, pp. 663-665.

74 Scharf, *Chronicles*, pp. 634-575; Smith, p. 290.

75 Theodore Roscoe, *The Web of Conspiracy*, (Prentice-Hall: 1959), pp. 90-91; Baley E. Marks and Mark N. Schatz, Ed., *Between North and South, A Maryland Journalist Views the Civil War*, (Fairleigh Dickerson Press: 1976), pp. 349-350.

[76] D.M. and P.B. Kunhardt, *Twenty Days*, (Castle Books: 1966), pp. 190-193.

[77] Ibid., p. 143; *Baltimore American*, April 22, 1865.

[78] Smith, pp. 317-320.

[79] R.D. Hunt and J.R. Brown, *Brevet Brigadier General in Blue*, (Olde Soldier Books: 1990), p. 693: Smith, p. 342; *The Sun* (Baltimore), February 1, 1866.

[80] *Report of the Ladies Southern Relief Association of Maryland, September 1st, 1866,* (Baltimore: 1866), p. 22; Schoeberlein, p. 484.

Chapter 5

[1] "[Monthly] Returns from U.S. Military Posts [Fort McHenry, 1841-1865]," M-617, Rolls 675-676, National Archives. Ezra J. Warner, *Generals in Blue: Lives of the Union Commanders*, (Louisiana University Press: 1988). See individual biographical listing of commanders.

[2] Ibid.

[3] Ibid.

[4] Ibid.

[5] Ibid.

[6] Ibid.

[7] Major Alfred Mordicai to Colonel H.K. Craig, May 25, 1857, "Letters Received, Office of the Chief of Ordnance," Records of the War Department, Record Group 92, National Archives.

[8] *The Sun* (Baltimore), May 25, 31, 1861.

[9] *The Sun* (Baltimore), June 4, 7, 8, 11, 1861.

[10] *The Sun* (Baltimore), July 2, 1861.

[11] Lt. Colonel William Brewerton to Brigadier General Joseph G. Totten, September 17, 1861, "Letters Received, Office of the Chief of U.S. Engineers," Record Group 77, National Archives.

[12] Major General John Dix to Colonel E.D. Townsend, Assistant Adjutant General, August 12, 1861, *Official Records of the War of the Rebellion* (Government Printing Office: 1899), Series 1, Vol. 5, p. 559. Hereafter cited as OR's.

[13] Captain J.D. Kurtz to Brigadier General Joseph G. Totten, June 20, 1861, "Letters Received, Office of the Chief of U.S. Engineers, " Record Group 77, National Archives. The letter was a result of the increased amounts of powder that was removed for security from the Pikesville Arsenal.

[14] "Abstracts from monthly returns of the principal U.S. military prisons," OR's, Series 2, Vol. 8, pp. 988-1002;

[15] Brigadier General William W. Morris to Colonel William Hoffman, September 14, 1863, OR's, Series 2, Vol. 6, p. 287. Hoffman's position was Commissary General of Prisoners.

[16] "Selected Records of the War Department Relating to Confederate Prisoners of War, 1861-1865," M-598, Roll 96 (Fort McHenry), National Archives. Hereafter cited as *Selected Records*.

[17] Morris to Hoffman, September 14, 1863.

[18] *"Selected Records."*; Transcript of a post war letter by Henry H. Brogan of his prison experiences at Fort McHenry, date unknown. Biographical Vertical Files-Fort McHenry Library.

[19] Morris to Hoffman, September 14, 1863.

20 "*Selected Records.*"; "State Prisoners Removed," *The Sun* (Baltimore), November 1, 1861; "Report of political prisoners taken, released and remaining since March 4, 1861, at Fort McHenry," Colonel William W. Morris to Major General John Dix, February 16, 1861. *OR's,* Series 2, Vol. 2, pp. 226-228..

21 Postmaster Montgomery Blair to Major General George McClellan (Enclosed in a letter from Major General John Dix to Blair, August 31, 1861), *OR's,* Series 2, Vol. 1, p. 591.

22 "*Abstracts*" and "*Selected Records.*"

23 "Engine Company No. 4 Oaths," Baltimore City Archives Records Center, Record Group 9, Nos. 1770-1779.

24 George McCaffrey to his wife Susan, July 27, 1861. Photo-copy in "McCaffrey Family Letters, "Biographical Vertical Files, Fort McHenry."; *The Sun* (Baltimore), April 27, July 25, 1862; "George McCaffrey - Refuses to take the oath of allegiance, but will give his parole not to aid or comfort the enemies of the United States Govt. Has taken his parole in Richmond .....Will take the oath." Henry McCaffrey - "Released by order of General [John] Wool, August 8, [1862] upon taking Special Order, Aug. 7, 1862. By order of Gen. Wool, not to take up arms against the U.S. Govt or in any manner either directly or indirectly, or abet the enemies thereof." "*Selected Records.*"

25 Ibid.

26 "*Selected Records.*"

27 Colonel P.A. Porter, 8th New York Artillery, commanding Fort McHenry, December 1863, *OR's* Series 2, Vol. 6, pp. 720-723.

28 Alexandria L. Levin, "A Wounded Confederate Soldier's Letter From Fort McHenry," *Maryland Historical Magazine* (Hereafter cited as MHM), Vol. 73, No. 4, December 1978, pp. 394-396; "*Selected Records.*"

29 Ibid.

30 Rev. Dr. T.D. Witherspoon, "Prison Life at Fort McHenry (Paper No. 2)," *Southern Historical Society Papers,* (Kraus Reprint Co.: New York: 1977), p 111. Dr. Witherspoon wrote three papers on his imprisonment at Fort McHenry. Hereafter cited as Witherspoon.

31 Colonel P.A. Porter, 8th New York Artillery, December 1863, *OR's,* Series 2, Vol. 6, pp. 721.

32 John O. Casler, *Four Years in the Stonewall Brigade,* (Morningside Bookshop, Publishers. Dayton, Ohio: 1971), p. 272. Casler belonged to Company A, 33rd Regiment Virginia Infantry. Hereafter cited as Casler.

33 Witherspoon, p. 115.

34 Casler, p. 281.

35 Casler, p. 282.

36 Witherspoon, p. 116.

37 John Dooley, *John Dooley, Confederate Soldier: His War Journal,* (Georgetown University Press: 1945), p. 124; Casler, p. 270; James T. Wells, "Prison Experience," *Southern Historical Society Papers,* (Kraus Reprint Co: 1977), Volume 7, January to December 1879, p. 324.

38 Kenneth W. Munden and Henry P. Beers, *The Union: A Guide to the Federal Archives Relating to the Civil War,* (National Archives and Records Administration, Washington: 1986), pp. 153-55, 319-320, 326.

39 "*Selected Records.*"

40 Colonel P.A. Porter, 8th New York Artillery, December 1863, *OR's,* Series 2, Vol. 6, p. 723.

41 *The Sun* (Baltimore), August 18, 24, 27,29, 1864.

[42] Private George Washington Kimball to wife, Maria, August 29, 1864. Photocopy at Fort McHenry Library, "Biographical Vertical Files." Kimball belonged to the "Mechanics Phalanx," that became Company G, Fifth Massachusetts Volunteer Militia.

[43] Isaac Markers, "Why President Lincoln Spared Three Lives," *The Confederate Veteran*, Vol. 19, 1911, p. 382.; Alfred S. Roe, *The Fifth Regiment Massachusetts Volunteer Infantry in its Three Tours of Duty, 1861, 1862-63, 1864*, (Fifth Regiment Veteran Association, Boston: 1911), p. 288; "*Selected Records.*"

[44] *The Sun* (Baltimore), March 8, 1862.

[45] Alfred Davenport, *Camp and Field Life of the Fifth New York Volunteer Infantry (Duryee Zouaves)*, (Dick and Fitzgerald, New York: 1879), p. 146.

[46] *The Sun* (Baltimore), January 14, May 24, 1864.

[47] "*Selected Records.*"

[48] *The Sun* (Baltimore), April 14, May 24, 1864; Roe, *The Fifth Regiment*, p.291-293.

[49] George W. Cullum, *Biographical Register of the Officers and Graduates of the U.S. Military Academy at West Point, N.Y.*, (D. Van Nostrand, New York: 1868), p. 210.

[50] Private Robert R. Moore to his mother, July 17, 1864. Kansas State Historical Center.

[51] John C. Myers, *A Daily Journal of the 192nd Regiment Pennsylvania Volunteers*, (Crissy & Markley, Printers, Philadelphia: 1864), pp. 23-40.

Chapter 6

[1] "Baltimore, and its Points of Attack and Defense," *The New York Tribune*, May 7, 1861.

[2] Morgan Dix, *Memoirs of John Adams Dix*, (Harper & Brothers, New York: 1888), pp. 24; Major General Dix to Major-General H.A. Halleck, September 15, 1862, *Memoirs*, p. 36.

[3] Major-General George B. McClellan to Brigadier-General Charles P. Stone (Division of the Potomac), August 18, 1861. *Official Records of the War of the Rebellion*, (Government Printing Office, Washington: 1881), Series 1, Vol. 5, p. 567. Hereafter cited as OR's.

[4] Daniel C. Toomey, *A History of Relay, Maryland and The Thomas Viaduct*, (Toomey Press: 1976), pp. 15-26.

[5] Alfred Davenport, *Camp and Field Life of the Fifth New York Volunteer Infantry (Duryee Zouaves)*, (Dick and Fitzgerald, New York: 1879), p. 105, 112.

[6] Lieutenant-Colonel Henry Brewerton to Major D.F. Van Buren, Assistant Adjutant- General, September 27, 1861, "Letters Received, Office of the Chief of U.S. Engineers," Record Group 77, National Archives.

[7] Lieutenant-Colonel Henry Brewerton to Major D.F. Van Buren, Assistant Adjutant- General, October 10, 1861, "Letters received, Office of the Chief of U.S. Engineers, RG 77, National Archives; Major-General John Dix to Colonel G.W. Cullum, Aide-de- Camp, HQ of the Army, August 17, 1861, OR's Series, 1, Vol. 5, pp. 565567. Hereafter cited as Dix to Cullum.

[8] Dix to Cullum.

[9] Ibid.

[10] Ibid.

[11] Ibid.

[12] Wilber Hunter, *Baltimore During the Civil War*, (The Board of Trustees of the Municipal Museum of the City of Baltimore (The Peale Museum): 1961), pp. 1-4.; Lois B. McCauley, *Maryland Historical Prints, 1752-1889*, (Maryland Historical Society, Baltimore: 1975), pp. 172, 182-209; Charles R. Harrison, "The Federal Occupation of Baltimore: A Survey of the Military Camp Locations, Troop Movements, and Unionist Sentiment in the City During the Civil War," (Unpublished study, University of Maryland, Baltimore County: April 29, 1983).

[13] Ibid.

[14] Ibid.

[15] Ibid.

[16] Major General Robert Schenck to Mayor Chapman, June 30, 1862. *OR's*, Series 1, Vol. 27, pp. 437-438.

[17] Ibid, p. 437; *Examiner* (Richmond, Virginia), December 31, 1863.

[18] "Report of the Defense Committee," October 28, 1864, Baltimore City Archives, Record Group 9, Series 2, Box 31, No. 73A. The Committee members were Mayor John L. Chapman, James Young, (President, First Branch), James C. Owen, (President, Second Branch), Robert M. Pround and J. Kernard; Captain William P. Craighill to Lt. Colonel B. Aluck, Assistant Adjutant General, December 18, 1865, and Captain Charles A. Turnbull to Lt. Colonel S.R. Lawrence, Assistant Adjutant General, May 4, 1865, "Letters Received, Office of the Chief of Engineers, " War Department, Record Group 77, National Archives; *OR's*, Series 1, Vol. 37, pp. 212- 216, 253; Franklin Cooling, *Jubal Early's Raid on Washington: 1864*, (Nautical and Aviation Publishing Company of America, Baltimore: 1995), pp. 157-176.

[19] Ibid.

[20] *The Sun* (Baltimore), July 15, 1864.

Chapter 7

[1] Robert I. Cottom, Jr., and Mary Ellen Hayward, *Maryland in the Civil War*, (Maryland Historical Society: 1994), p. 33.

[2] Isaac M. Fein, *Baltimore Jews During the Civil War*, (American Jewish Historical Quarterly, Vol. 51, No. 2: December 1961), pp. 68-69.

[3] M. Ray Della, Jr., "An Analysis of Baltimore's Population in 1850," *Maryland Historical Magazine*, Vol. 68, No. 1, Spring 1973, p. 21. Hereafter cited as *MHM*.

[4] Hamilton Owens, *Baltimore on the Chesapeake*, (Doubleday, Doran and Company: 1941), pp. 281, 292.

[5] Ibid., pp. 284-285.

[6] *The Sun* (Baltimore), October 20, 26, 28, 1861.

[7] *The Sun* (Baltimore), November 19, 23, 1861.

[8] William N. Still, *USS Monitor*, (National Maritime Initiative: 1988), p. 12.

[9] *The Sun* (Baltimore), October 4, 1861, December 15, 1864, and May 5, 1865; *Official Records of the War of the Rebellion* (Hereafter cited as *OR's*.), U.S. Navy Series 2, Vol. 1, pp. 149, 179, 238.

[10] William I. Kelly, "Baltimore Steamboats in the Civil War," *MHM*, 37, No. 1, March 1942, pp. 42-43, 46.

[11] *OR's* U.S. Navy, Series 2, Vol. 1, pp. 171, 234.

[12] William Pierce to Major General John Dix, August 13, 1861. "Selected Letters Received, Office of the Quartermaster General," War Department, Record Group 92, National Archives.

[13] Jay Slagle, Ironclad Captain, (Kent State University Press: 1996), p. 122; Owens, p. 282.

[14] The Sun (Baltimore), November __, 1861; Arcadi Gluckman, United States Muskets, Rifles and Carbines, (Otto Ulbrich Company, Inc., New York: 1948), pp. 264-265, 390-393.

[15] Owens, p. 290.

[16] L.A. Wilmer, History and Roster of Maryland of Maryland Volunteers, War of 1861-1865, Volumes 1, (Baltimore: 1898), . See history of each unit for location where companies were recruited and regiments were mustered for service. Hereafter cited as Wilmer.

[17] Scharf, Chronicles, p. 627; Wilmer, Vol. 1, p. 460.

[18] Wilmer, Vol. 1, pp. 336, 353, 375.

[19] Wilmer, Vol. 2, pp. 129, 155, 261.

[20] Lois B. McCauley, Maryland Historical Prints, 1752-1889, (Maryland Historical Society, Baltimore: 1975), p. 206; U.S. Christian Commission, Second Report of the Committee of Maryland, (Baltimore: 1863), p. 69. Hereafter cited as Second Report.

[21] McCauley, p. 203; Second Report, pp. 62-63.

[22] McCauley, pp. 194-195, 207; Second Report, pp. 42, 77.

[23] McCauley, pp. 191, 196-197; Second Report, p. 55.

[24] Second Report, pp. 37, 39, 53, 76-77.

[25] Andrew B. Cross, The War, Battle of Gettysburg and the Christian Commission, (Baltimore: 1865), p. 24.

$\mathcal{I}$NDEX